SIGHT, SOUND, AND SUNSHINE

D1292960

SIGHT, SOUND, AND SUNSHINE

TAMPA, HELL HARBOR, AND THE MAKING OF MODERN CINEMA

KEVIN J. MARTINEZ

Library of Congress Control Number: 2019957285
ISBN: 978-0-578-62192-0
E-book: 978-0-578-93273-6

DEDICATED
TO

Joseph and Mary Martinez

1

IN the later part of the 1920s Tampa, Florida was starting to stretch as a city; the first high rise appeared on the skyline when the luxurious 19 story Hotel Floridan opened its doors, the vast expanse of West Tampa had been annexed, and plans were being drawn up to build a ten mile causeway over the bay that would connect Clearwater in Pinellas County on the eastern side of Tampa Bay to Hillsborough County on the west. The city's fame as the cigar capital of the United States would also be confirmed, yet again, when the half-billionth cigar was rolled in 1929. What else, the 100,000 residents of the burgeoning city wondered, could possibly illuminate Tampa more than these accomplishments?

At the same time, the motion picture industry was also undergoing a profound change. In 1927, Warner Brothers released *The Jazz Singer*; a mostly silent film that strategically incorporated sound to the musical numbers of its star, Al Jolson. Despite a running time of 90 minutes, of which only 15 minutes has recorded sound, *The Jazz Singer* ignited an explosion that reverberated worldwide and altered forever the way movies were presented to the public. The synchronization of sound to action was the single greatest cinematic innovation since the camera; adding a new, aural dimension to the visual medium. Before the end of Jolson's first song, the death knell for silent movies began to ring, and in less than two years, silent features were interred into a cultural time capsule that would define a bygone era.

Between 1927 and 1929 dialogue was starting to be heard in films. Most movies were generally still silent, but they were beginning to intersperse a few scenes of dialogue or musical soundtracks into each production. In July of 1928, Warner Brothers released *Lights of New York*, the first all-talking picture. On January 20, 1929, Fox-Movietone presented *In Old Arizona*, an adaptation of O. Henry's short story *The Caballero's Way*, which also introduced the Cisco Kid, and became the first movie with sound to be filmed mostly, but not entirely, on location. The future of modern cinema was on the march. Sound was dramatically enhancing the ability to tell a story, and no filmmaker was as ready to exploit the new technology more than Henry King; a meticulous director with a penchant for literary adaptations, and a reputation for recognizing talent.

King was born in rural Christianburg, Virginia in 1886. He started out as traveling stage performer finally making his film debut in 1913, but by 1915 his interest shifted to directing. Seeking more creative control over his work, he co-founded Inspiration Pictures with actor Richard Barthelmes and producer Charles Duell. Inspiration Pictures was established in 1921 as an independent production company that would make films for United Artists. It was King, however, who was the technical heart of the company, and his skill behind the camera led to a string of successful films for Inspiration, among them: *Tol'able David* and the original *Stella Dallas*. In his 1929 film, *She Goes to War*, the director included a few bits of recorded dialogue. He recognized that sound, if used correctly, could take movies to new heights, and for him, movies were the natural progression of storytelling. King also believed that motion pictures were just as important as schools and churches for conveying knowledge and messages. The audience's ability to hear mood-setting music, conversations, and soliloquies along with well-told stories might just be the catalyst needed to elevate cinema into a higher art form rather than a simple form of plebian entertainment.

The director also wanted to make motion pictures where not only sound but places would play a major role. Many silent films had used foreign and exotic locales as backgrounds. King's 1923 film, *The White Sister* starring Lillian Gish was made in Italy with the enthusiastic permission of Benito Mussolini. The new audio equipment of 1929 however, was cumbersome and prohibited on location shooting. It was far more feasible to use indoor soundstages that prevented interference from wind and background noise; as well as giving the sound engineers the ability to hide microphones close enough to the actors in order to capture their voices. Despite a myriad of reasons not to shoot on location, Henry King's vision of the modern movie would not be halted simply because technology could not catch up. He wanted to produce a movie that would bring together the biggest names in silent film and deliver their unheard acting talents to the public. This film, he believed, would be a one-way bridge between "silents" and "talkies" and would help redefine cinema forever. To achieve this, he would need a story with interesting characters, set in a scenic place, and doing dramatic things. For this endeavor, he selected a 1925 novel, set partially in the West Indies, called *Out of the Night* by Rida Johnson Young.

2

AS wordsmiths go, the author of *Out of the Night*, Rida Johnson-Young, was one of the most prolific. Although she only wrote four novels during her lifetime; she is remembered as playwright, librettist, and songwriter whose name shined as bright on the marquees of Broadway as her contemporary, George M. Cohan. During a career that spanned a mere fifteen years, she wrote nearly thirty plays and over 500 musical compositions for the stage. Her work as a collaborative lyricist with Victor Herbert produced the exuberant *Ah! Sweet Mystery of Life* for the light opera *Naughty Marietta*, and the sentimental Irish-American standard, *Mother Machree* for her own play, *Barry of Ballymore* in partnership with the songwriting team of Chauncey Olcott and Ernest Ball. So important and vast is her musical catalog, that she was selected as one of the first inductees into the Songwriters Hall of Fame when it was established in 1970.

Despite her successful career in the legitimate theatre, she was no stranger to the movie business and its advancements. Johnson-Young saw a number of her plays adapted for the screen, and in 1919, she penned a now lost photoplay called *The Little Boss*. In 1928 her book, *The Story of Mother Machree* was made into a motion picture by John Ford and featured a synchronized disk soundtrack where the title song was played throughout.

Her novel *Out of the Night*, tells the story of Asta

Morgan: a sixteen-year-old girl who lives on the West Indian island of Abaco in the 1920s. The fictionalized version of the Bahamian Island is populated by the descendants of the notorious pirate Captain Morgan, where under tropical skies they live dissolute lives of copious drinking and inbreeding. When they are not stealing from one another, they plunder the occasional tourist by overcharging for worthless trinkets. They hold proud to their buccaneer pedigree, which for them justifies their behavior, but as the generations have left them with little outside contact, they have drifted into a sea of self-resignation and personal apathy.

Asta however, is different. She is the product of a Castilian mother and a father who is a direct descendant of the pirate Morgan. She yearns to leave the island and visit Havana where "handsome men rode about in carriages with ladies in fine lace." Unfortunately, she is promised in marriage to her cousin Joseph on her seventeenth birthday. When Asta is caught by her father and Joseph in a flirtatious act with the local bad boy, Anthony Horngold, the wedding date is moved up. It is at this moment a wealthy American named Bob Wade arrives on the island with his friends on their yacht. The vivacious girl is attracted to the older, ennui plagued playboy and stows away on the yacht which is headed for Nassau. When the also smitten Wade discovers her on board, he hides her and breaks the news to the ship's owners the next morning once they are too far from Abaco to return. Wade returns with his friends to The United States, leaving Asta in the Bahamian capital under the care of a gentlewoman named Miss Farnham who is asked to educate the feral girl in the civilized manners of society. Lost in the new city, stifled by the constraints of formal education, and determined to see Havana on her way to a hopeful reunification with Bob Wade, Asta escapes.

The novel then becomes a circuitous odyssey of self-discovery and a meditation on guilt, forgiveness, and class difference. Asta finally makes it to Havana where she weds a wealthy landowner. Later, during an ocean trip with her husband, their ship is destroyed at sea by a hurricane and the nearly drowned newlywed wife awakes on a Florida beach, and finds herself a widow. Eventually, Asta winds up in New York where she is reunited with Wade and enters high society, but a devastating fall from grace forces her to re-examine herself. In the end, she discovers that she can never be a part of the small world she once sought because there is an even more important place for her in the wider universe.

Sadly, the finished screenplay would lack the breadth and scope of the original book, becoming a re-imagined adaptation of its first forty pages. On its own, however, the screenplay holds up quite well as a distinct story. The writing team wisely decided to change the heroine's name to Anita but unfortunately chose to focus the story solely on her life as an island girl. The island's name of Abaco is renamed Madre for the film, but the new appellative only appears on the paper script; at no time in the film is the small dominion ever called by a proper name.

The movie begins when a handful of pearls are sold to the local trader Joseph Horngold by a man named Peg Leg written into the script. Later, when Peg Leg is murdered by

Anita's father in an attempt to rob him, Horngold witnesses the act thus allowing the sleazy merchant to negotiate for Anita's hand in exchange for his silence. Neither the deal nor the marriage, however, can be consummated until the pearls are sold to the American trader Bob Wade who is about to visit the island. Anita meets Wade while attempting to stop the sale and finds herself falling in love with him.

Characters would be changed and added for the film. The movie character of Joseph Horngold would be a merger of the book's Tony Horngold; a virile, handsome thief with whom Asta flirts, and Joseph Morgan; her rich, facially deformed, land owning cousin to whom she is promised in marriage. The merged character, now named Joseph Horngold, is a rich trader with a deforming scar down his face whom Anita is being forced to marry.

Bob Wade in the novel is a playboy sailing through the Caribbean with friends, but on film, he is transformed into a merchant trader that comes to port with the intention of buying pearls. His crew includes his first mate Bunion and a Black sailor named Nemo, who is portrayed by a Tampa man named Ulysses Williams. Wade rescues Anita and the two sail off into presumably future wedded bliss with a chorus of happy sailors heralding the event in song. The final scenes end the film where the book begins in earnest. The heroine of Johnson-Young's novel has a much different conclusion to her story, and while there may not be singing seamen, the reader is left to believe that her life will be a happy one.

Rida Johnson-Young would never see the adaptation of

Into the Night. She died on May 8, 1926, at her Stamford, Connecticut home of cancer. She was only fifty-one.

Turning a book into a movie required the services of three writers. The Scenarist: who wrote a brief description of the story for the producers and the directors; making changes to the story for its feasibility as a film. The Screenwriter: would then adapt the scenario given to them, delivering the final literary product and telling the story the way the director should complete it. As sound came to the movies, an additional Screenwriter was needed to supply dialogue.

N. Brewster Morse would write the scenario. He had been a prolific writer since the age of eleven and a talented son of privilege with a familial genealogy that went back to the earliest English and Dutch settlers in the United States. Included in his lineage was: New York Supreme Court Justice Nathan Brewster Morse, for whom he was named, and his wife Eliza Tiffany, sister of the founder of the famous jewelry store, Tiffany and Company.

Morse was a published poet, and in one year during the 1920s, it was estimated that he had written the verse in 46% of the greeting cards on the market. He also wrote and drew syndicated cartoons serials based on classic literature. Morse traveled to Hollywood around 1920, and by 1921 two of his screenplays would be produced: *His Brother's Keeper*, a story dealing with the subject of mind control and murder, and *The Crimson Cross,* a detective drama. He later returned to the East Coast and continued to write. 1926 saw his play, *The Half Naked Truth,* a comedy about a male model's reluctant fame; have its Broadway debut, running for 38 performances at the Mayfair Theater.

A few years later, Morse would try his hand at directing a remake of the 1916 motion picture *The Strength of the Weak* on location in his hometown of Milford, Pennsylvania. Morse also insisted that the movie have its premiere in Milford where a number of its residents had parts including his sister, Katherine Morse in the lead role. Other stars included Broadway actor Douglas Wood; screen actor, William P. Carelton, and someone that could be considered one of the world's first movie celebrities, Augustus Phillips, who appeared in many of Thomas Edison's earliest experimental films. While the original version of *The Strength of the Weak* is familiar to film historians, the Morse version has, it seems, been lost.

Frederique Rosine de Gresac who went by the professional name of Fred de Gresac, was hired to adapt the novel. The noted French journalist turned composer and playwright began her writing career in Paris. She shortened the feminine Frederique to the masculine Fred at the urging of the Parisian theater managers who insisted that a woman could never be accepted as a playwright. She often recounted the sad story of how, after the conclusion of her first play, the audience called for the author while she remained seated among the confused crowd; quietly failing to take the credit for fear of a backlash.

She would arrive in Hollywood on the wings of a successful Broadway career that included *The Marriage of Kitty* (an Americanization of her French play *La Passerelle)*, and *Sweethearts,* which later featured the singing duo of

Jeanette MacDonald and Nelson Eddy for the 1938 film version. De Gresac began working as a screenwriter and brought to film Alexandre Dumas' *Camille*, Henri Murger's *La Boheme,* and a sequel to Rudolph Valentino's immortal character the Sheik in *Son of the Sheik*. Once at work, de Gresac developed a name that became so influential in Hollywood that she would maintain her own suite of offices at MGM throughout the silent era. In 1928 she was asked to adapt the scenario by Howard Estabrook that would become *She Goes to War*, the following year Henry King asked her to adapt *Out of the Night*.

Clarke Silvernail: a former actor and director of Broadway plays for the Shubert brothers would be assigned to write the scenes and dialogue for the film. Silvernail was well known in theatrical circles for his active participation in Actor's Equity where he held the position of Councilman. He was an early show business volunteer to military service in the Hospital Corps during World War I where he also arranged entertainment for the wounded. After the war, he returned to the theater continuing to write and direct. In 1929 he helped adapt the play *Cafe de Danse* for the Broadway stage and then headed west to Hollywood to work as a screenwriter.

After a number of meetings, drafts, and rewrites which would continue well into the production; the screenplay for King's film would take its final shape. It would also go through a few name changes along the way as well: from the original screen title; *The Blood of the Buccaneer,* to the book's original title *Out of the Night,* to a mistakenly juvenile sounding *The Little Pirate,* a term Bob Wade calls Anita in one scene, and finally to the perhaps overly ominous, *Hell Harbor* as the final choice.

3

ONCE the financing for the project had been secured; King went looking for a tropical setting to film his opus, but after months of personally traversing the coastal regions of the American south, he was unable to find the perfect location. King shared his frustrations during a conversation with his old friend, the actor Thomas Meighan; who suggested that King might find what he was looking for on Florida's West Coast. Meighan was well acquainted with the area because he owned a vacation home in the sleepy town of New Port Richey; some fifty miles to the northwest of Tampa. The harried director took his friend's advice and visited the Sunshine State.

On his trip, King discovered Rocky Point; a narrow, privately owned barrier island situated in Tampa Bay and located on the periphery of Hillsborough County with a small road connecting it to the mainland. The site, which was used as a public beach by day and place for young lovers' trysts by night, was undeveloped and provided a lush tropical setting including a natural harbor that could pass as a Caribbean port with a little help from Hollywood. The location was easily accessible to the city center, but still far enough to afford the necessary privacy needed for filming. King had at last found his location and immediately began a charm offensive; contacting Trenton Collins, Publicity Manager of the Tampa Chamber of Commerce, along with city leaders for indications of interest regarding the production. It was Milton Mabry's indulgence however, that was most sought after. As the owner of Rocky Point, he held the use of paradise in his hands. His acquiescence was memorialized in a deal that allowed the use of the island for a specific time, and the prohibition of any other filmmakers before spring.

At the time, Tampa was actually two distinct cities: The central government rested in downtown, but over ten percent of the population lived in the immigrant and ethnic stronghold section of town nicknamed Ybor City. Originally an enclave founded by Spaniards and Cubans that came to work in the cigar factories in the late 1800s, by the turn of the century a large influx of Italians had arrived along with a distinct representation of Germans.

Ybor City was named after Vincente Martinez Ybor, a Spanish industrialist who was born in Valencia, Spain and operated a cigar factory in Cuba. Ybor brought cigar manufacturing to Tampa in 1885 on the advice of his friend, and fellow Spaniard, Gabino Gutierrez after revolutionary fervor gripped the island. By 1886, Vincente Ybor had the largest cigar factory in the world and Gutierrez, an American educated civil engineer, planned and shaped the factory town. The industry gave worldwide recognition to Tampa and made its name synonymous with cigars. By the 1920s, tobacco had created a kingdom in what was once the scrub brush and desolation that surrounded the city center. The Mayor of Tampa, D.B. McKay and his wife Aurora, could have easily claimed the unofficial title of Tampa's royal family.

He was a descendant of one of the area's first settlers and she was the daughter of Gabino Gutierrez.

Although the city was small in comparison to other metro areas, Tampa did have some big problems with crime and corruption and often the two went together. When Luther Hatton ran for Hillsborough County Sheriff as a law and order man in 1928, there were criminal elements that attempted to thwart his candidacy. On Election Day of that year, unidentified gunmen charged into the Hyde Park suburb polling place with guns blazing and attempted to steal the ballot box. The precinct was an area where Hatton had considerable support. Two people were wounded in the shootout, but the ballot box was retrieved undamaged after a brief chase. Hatton won the election with the overwhelming support of Tampa's women, but he would later be removed from office on the grounds of malfeasance and misfeasance by Florida's Governor Doyle Carlton. His term in office was a mere nine months.

Many believe that Hatton's dismissal was politically motivated and that some of the charges leveled against him were exaggerated. His legal challenges and a second run for office in 1940 were unsuccessful. He continued to work in Tampa's law enforcement until he died in 1965.

Donald Brenham McKay was serving the first year of his third term as Mayor. In his first two terms (1910-1920) he focused on municipal improvements: sidewalks were laid, the city streets were paved, the first library was built, and an expanded sewer system was put in place. When he ran for office again in 1928, his focus became the enhancement of the city's commercial appeal. Tampa was easily accessible thanks to the railroad established by Henry Plant in the last century that made it ideal for commerce and tourism. The city could also boast about its small but growing seaport that had once ferried soldiers to Cuba during the Spanish American War but was now engaged in the profitability of peaceful maritime shipments. The land boom on Florida's eastern coast had come to a screeching halt after a massive hurricane destroyed property, made the Miami Harbor impassible by sinking a ship in it, and halted rail lines. Northern eyes, however, were still looking for warmer climates in which to vacation and McKay began to see Tampa as the natural alternative to the void that had been created. While it had the attributes of climate, commerce, and convenience; Tampa needed to be seen.

The area had made appearances in films before. In 1898 a number of short films called "actualities" were shot by the Edison Manufacturing Company and its rival, The American Mutoscope Company showing troops in the city preparing for the Cuban Campaign. These were single events with titles like *10th Infantry Disembarking from Cars, The 69th Regiment Passing in Review,* and *The 9th Infantry Boys' Morning Wash.* Actualities were precursors to the modern documentary, and while these short films had their place in history, by 1929, movies had progressed. The medium was now making stars out of talent simply because they were seen by larger audiences. In short: a film could promote as well as entertain.

As the publisher of the Tampa Daily Times newspaper; D.B. McKay understood the power and rewards of advertising, so when the suggestion that a major motion picture would like to use the area's tropical splendor as a backdrop, the mayor would not only give his resounding support to the project but would also rally the business community of the city and all the political powers of the state to make it happen.

4

AFTER receiving positive affirmations from Tampa, Henry King arrived with an advance production team that also included his brother Louis King, also a director; the former silent film actor Harry Ham, and a young assistant director named Richard Harlan who would later find his niche directing Spanish language versions of American movies in the 1930's and 1940's.

Carl Brorien, Sr., Vice President of the local telephone company and President of the Chamber of Commerce took an active role in supporting the film. Under his leadership, the Chamber provided office space for the executives and logistical help when needed. The Chamber's public relations officer, Trenton Collins would work closely with Inspiration Pictures to promote the project. Tampa's main contribution to the project, however, was found in the currency of its appointed ambassadors; average citizens who helped with everything from providing local advice to serving a home cooked meal for the advance team.

Once settled, Henry King dispatched designer Robert Haas to Rocky Point with instructions to build a set. As a graduate of the University of Pennsylvania's architecture program, the Newark, New Jersey native had worked almost exclusively in the film business after graduation. His reputation for aesthetics was well regarded both within the industry and by King with whom he had worked for previously. By

1929, Robert Haas had built and designed sets for nineteen silent features in the first ten years of his career. His plans for this film called for the construction of actual buildings that would resemble a dilapidated West Indian port town. All of the structures, like the El Marino Cafe, would also include finished rooms so that interior shots could be filmed without using a studio soundstage. The buildings would all have roofs placed atop them in order to block the disruption of outside sounds and inclement weather. The entire set would be built on the southern side of Rocky Point with the towering remnants of a castle keep at the western tip of the island which would be the home of Henry Morgan and his daughter, Anita in the film.

As contractors began working, two young men showed up on August 28, 1929, to find work on the construction crew building the set at Rocky Point. What made their particular story noteworthy is that they traveled from California: walking, hitchhiking and sleeping in haylofts the entire way. Twenty-year-old Joe Halloran had worked at various jobs in the movie industry since starting as a property boy at the age of ten. He had just finished working on the set of the silent film, *Evangeline* starring Delores del Rio and was fascinated by the notion of a sound film in production. Seeking to be a part of the new technological advancement, Halloran and his friend Leonard Gwynne, made a fourteen-day trek across America and presented themselves to King. Gwynne was given a job as a carpenter while Halloran was assigned to the sound unit.

Second Assistant Director, Bob Brandt was charged with

assembling a flotilla of boats which would be anchored in various parts of the harbor. The task was easy enough, given that Tampa was a port city and the neighboring municipalities of Clearwater and St. Petersburg were populated with watercraft owners of all types. His toughest job, however, was finding a ship big enough for Bob Wade's merchant vessel. On September 17, 1929, Brandt managed to deliver a double mast, 15- ton schooner named Elsie.

The Elsie had a long legacy on the waters of Tampa and the Caribbean. It alternated as a merchant cargo ship; visiting ports of call in Trinidad and Martinique, but mostly it served as a fishing ship. The vessel would eventually be purchased by Sabastiano Mirabella, an Italian immigrant from Catania, Sicily who owned a large fish market in Tampa. In April of 1929, it was sold at a public auction to help settle the estate of Mirabella.

The most colorful character of the production was not an actor, but rather its property manager, Count Phillip d'Esco. d'Esco was a member of the royal court of Romania, and like much of Europe's royalty after WWI, he had fallen on hard financial times. He left Europe after the war and settled in the United States. Hiding his old world pedigree, he obtained work as a property man at one of the small studios in California and was known by his colleagues simply as Phil. His true identity was revealed when a cable was delivered to him on set and addressed to Count Phillip.

"While I am in exile, I don't feel like an outcast." He once stated. "When I walk among the magnificent sets you Americans construct at such great expense...I imagine that I am back in my own country. With the California climate and the Romanian castles around me... I am happier than I have ever been in my life."

In 1925 he attempted to negotiate a motion picture contract for the recently abdicated Romanian King, Carol II, and his mistress Elena Lupescu. The King had renounced his right to the throne to be with Lupescu, and d'Esco had approached a number of producers about featuring the now cash-strapped ex-monarch and his lover in a motion picture. The offers, however, were soundly rejected.

In 1929, he obtained employment with director Herbert Brenon on his film *Sorrell and Son* as a property manager. Brenon, later hired by United Artists, was so impressed with d'Esco's vast knowledge of antiques and architecture that he rehired him in 1927 for his film *Lummox*. The Count would eventually be asked by Henry King to manage props for *Hell Harbor*.

5

ON September 1, 1929, shortly after Haas had completed the set, but before the arrival of the cast and the beginning of principal photography; Inspiration Pictures and United Artists hosted a party for Mayor McKay and Tampa's political elite. The Board of Aldermen and the County Commissioners were all in attendance along with judges, the newly elected Sheriff, Luther Hatton, and members of the Chamber of Commerce. For King, it was a way to say thank you for the city's hospitality, and for the city, it was a victory celebration. Tampa had beat out the neighboring towns of Tarpon Springs, New Port Richey, Sarasota, and Venice to become the place that satisfied the director's vision for his innovative motion picture.

The day consisted of a tour of the structures, with lectures by architect Robert Haas. Property Manager, Alberto d'Agustino, who had been responsible for procuring many of the props, talked about traveling to New Orleans, Havana, and nearby Tarpon Springs to purchase antique grills and shutters for the buildings. Walter Jacobson, the chief plasterer demonstrated for the audience how he created the building facades using cement, glue, and horsehair.

The Diana Sextette, a Cuban son band from Havana, entertained the guests while a buffet lunch was served in the El Marino Cafe. The studio's publicity man, Lou Lusty served as the Master of Ceremonies in place of Henry King, who had returned to California.

The honored guests sat in numbed awe of their hosts and their surroundings. As they breathed in the scent of newly completed construction and paint; Mayor McKay, the Chamber of Commerce President Carl D. Brorein, Sr., and other members of the municipal government in attendance must have felt their hearts swelling with pride at each platitude given by the production executives. Countless times they sat across tables for long hours debating and planning Tampa's future; always looking for ways to use its resources with the outcome of making it a place of progress and civility. Now, at this moment, the future came to them in the light of images and the thunderclap of sound. The city's investment in the project had paid off and its dividends could be endless. The economy of Tampa would immediately reap many financial benefits resulting from the estimated $290,000.00 production.

It was also announced at the luncheon that between 125 and 250 local extras would be hired at a maximum rate of $7.50 per day. All props and equipment would also be purchased locally whenever possible, and in one week, Henry King would return to Tampa, arriving by train with the stars of the film. Shooting would begin Monday, November 9th, as scheduled.

The dream had become a reality for the city fathers who had helped shepherd the production to Tampa; now they knew that they must become stewards of the dream to build on it. Some of cinema's most notable names were coming to

Tampa, and Tampa would pull out all of the stops to make sure that their stay was enjoyable, hospitable, and most importantly, a reason to return.

One of the selling points of shooting in Tampa was the ability to have luxurious accommodations to retreat to at the end of the day, and the Hotel Floridan was that place of refuge. Opened two years earlier, on January 29, 1927, the Floridan was the brainchild of a Canadian developer named Allan J. Simms who came to Tampa in 1906. After a while, Simms saw the need for a well-appointed hotel in the city and acquired a corner lot downtown. He then hired the architectural firm of Francis J. Kennard & Sons of Tampa to design the stately building, while G.A. Miller, Inc. was in charge of the construction.

The hotel stood 240 feet tall making it the tallest building in all of Florida and it would retain that title until 1966 when the Exchange Bank building was constructed a few blocks down the street. The Floridan cost a total of $3,000,000.00 to build and decorate. The interior was appointed with the finest furnishings money could buy. It also boasted of an all gas kitchen with electrical refrigeration. The main dining room and coffee shop employed sixty-five people and the French-trained executive chef, James Kaller, had previously served in the same capacity to the Ottoman Sultan of Egypt, Kamil Pasha Khedive.

The most unique feature in the structure's design was a drive-in garage that allowed guests to pull their cars into the building where an elevator was available for their luggage; the elevator led to the Bellman's area for delivery to the guest's room. By creating this special entrance for the loading and unloading of suitcases, the traffic on Cass and Florida Streets which bordered the hotel allowed the street traffic to continue flowing unimpeded and prevented guest baggage from being placed on the outside sidewalk.

On September 17, 1929, the Tampa Daily Times ran an advertisement placed by the Chamber of Commerce. The new sheriff, Luther Hatton also made a contribution to its publication along with many of the city's leading businesses. The double page ad served two purposes: First, to welcome Henry King and his stable of stars whose publicity stills liberally graced the announcement, and more importantly, to implore the citizenry of Tampa to support the success of the picture by suggesting that each person write ten letters to "friends in the north" encouraging them to see the movie when it comes to their town. Directions were given to explain to them how well the picture depicts the natural beauty of the area. By doing this, Tampans would show their gratitude in a tangible way to the production, extol the beauty of their home, and ultimately bring more films to the area. The artistic value of the first all-talking picture, shot entirely on location, was guaranteed by Henry King and the talent he employed; the success of the picture was dependent on everyone else.

6

A S the leadership of Tampa feasted from the movie set buffet; Henry King was in California organizing the cast for travel and seeing to it that the proper equipment was loaded onto the train. He was also there for what appears to be either damage control or image building. A few days earlier, the newswires reported that Lupe Velez had suffered a nervous breakdown and that her arrival to the Florida film set would be delayed indefinitely. Whether this ailment was a legitimate medical crisis or a well thought out publicity stunt is a matter of speculation. It is a well- known fact that the actress suffered from mood swings that became more violent over time, and some of her biographers have surmised that she may have even had a bipolar disorder. The cause of her breakdown was reported to have been brought on by over-work and long periods on a poorly ventilated sound stage while filming *Tiger Rose*.

Immediately after the initial report, Velez spoke to reporters as to how surprised she was to read of her break-down. She denied the allegation and said that she was still working on finishing her latest film; she was not, as reported, bedridden. To further confirm her vitality: the mother of her intended fiancé, Gary Cooper stated that she had lunch with the actress earlier in the week and that Miss Velez was appeared to be fine.

The timing of such news is suspect and may have been

manufactured as a way to elevate the star power of *Hell Harbor's* leading lady. In show business there is an old adage: "Keep them wanting more" and the population of Tampa wanted nothing more than Lupe Velez.

Velez had been a Vaudeville star in her native Mexico; a singer, dancer, and comedienne with a talent for raucous imitations of other show business counterparts. She was both beautiful and irrepressible and she created for U.S. audiences the original persona of the fiery Latin American woman that was full of high energy and a vocabulary of innocent malapropisms —a persona that was not too far from the personality of the actress. Her *Hell Harbor* co-star, John Holland would later remark:

"Clara Bow may have "It" but only Lupe can entertain a whole 24 hours of the day without anyone helping her."

After being in Hollywood for only two years she had appeared in two short films for Hal Roach and six motion pictures; working opposite some of the biggest names in comedy and drama: Laurel and Hardy, Douglas Fairbanks, and Gary Cooper — with whom she became romantically involved. Before joining the *Hell Harbor* cast, Velez had just completed a talking picture called *Tiger Rose,* featuring another movie veteran of more than twenty films: Rin Tin Tin.

From the moment it was announced that she was coming to Tampa, the city experienced a mass ecstatic episode. Lou Lusty referred to it later as "Lupeness". Local songwriters wrote songs about her, and largely untalented rhymers submitted laudatory verses in wildly amateurish iambic pentameter for the poetry corner of the local newspapers; extolling the beauty and personality of a woman they had never met.

Already well known to the movie going public, and particularly admired by the Spanish speaking residents of the city, the actress would find an enormous community of fans that became transfixed by her presence. Any news that Lupe might not come to Tampa only added exponentially to their desire to see her. When the supposed crisis had passed and she finally did arrive, the girl from San Luis Potosi, Mexico would witness a fanatical outpouring of joy and adulation. To the people of Tampa, Lupe Velez was not just a star she was a supernova whose light shined greater than that of all of her co-stars' combined. The always astute Henry King recognized this phenomenon and went to great lengths to ensure that his film's leading lady would be treated in a manner that stressed her importance. He saw to it that the city of Tampa sprayed insecticide on the beach to prevent mosquitoes and sand flies from biting her, and she was given one of the set's buildings to use as a private dressing room. King also directed multiple scenes with long close-ups that not only exploited her pulchritude, but her emoting abilities as well. Cinematographers John Fulton and Mack Stengler showed that Lupe did not just photograph well, she made love to the camera and the camera, in turn, loved her back. Off-screen, King deliberately allowed her to take center stage at any public gatherings.

7

FOR *Hell Harbor*, King would reteam Gibson Gowland and Jean Herscholt who played antagonists in Erich von Stroheim's epic film *Greed*. The two would once again play morally corrupt men with a disdain for each other that are brought together and eventually destroyed by their personal flaws and avarice. Gowland would perform the role of Henry Morgan, the seedy and abusive father of a beautiful daughter whom he agrees to sell into marriage in exchange for the money and silence of the equally deplorable Joseph Horngold, portrayed by Hersholt,

John Holland's part would be that of Bob Wade, the dashing romantic interest who comes to the island as a trader and falls in love with Anita. The role was perfect for Holland, who loved the sea so much that he ran away from boarding school to join the Navy. He had also been in Tampa years earlier, gaining employment as a boiler stoker onboard a ship heading to South America. The ship entered a watery grave somewhere in the Caribbean and the crew had to be rescued.

Breaking into show business was just as difficult for Holland as shoveling coal. He decided to attend the Lasky School for Amateurs, and his good looks caught the eye of a female scout who arranged a movie audition for him. His performance that day was so bad he was advised to seek another line of work. The repudiation of his acting skills, he would later recount, got his "Irish up" and he the struggling actor took small roles in any theater production he could find in order to hone his craft. In 1926 he auditioned for the legendary film pioneer Allan Dwan and won a role in his film *Summer Bachelors*. This was followed by two more films in 1927; *Rich but Honest*, and *Secret Studio*. He was billed as Clifford Holland in these early films and just as his career appeared to be taking off, the actor began to suffer a series of setbacks which included a severe allergic reaction to studio makeup, a nervous breakdown, and a brain hemorrhage that forced him to leave films for a short time. He believed that his acting days were over until Henry King hired him as the leading man in *She Goes to War*.

A brief but pivotal role in *Hell Harbor* was that of an added character named Peg Leg, played by Australian born Harry Allen. Additional characters would be written into the screenplay like Blinky; a storytelling Irish beachcomber portrayed by Paul Burns and his young sidekick Spotty who has a boyhood crush on Anita, played by George Bookasta.

Gibson Gowland was fifty-two years old when he arrived in Tampa and was an imposingly big man both in physical stature and reputation. He had been an adventurer; leaving his comfortable home in Spennymoor, England to see the world as a sailor, then disembarking at some point on the African continent where he led safaris, worked as a diamond miner, and founded a theatrical company in Johannesburg. Never content to stay in one place; Gibson immigrated to Canada, where he met and married a fellow English expatriate eighteen years his junior, named Beatrice Bird who had dreams of acting and writing. The newlyweds moved to

California to be in motion pictures and found work in small roles. One of Gibson's first appearances on film was a small part in D.W. Griffith's *Birth of a Nation.* Beatrice acted in a photoplay based on one of her own short stories titled, *The Small Magnetic Hand.* Once in Hollywood, Beatrice would adopt the name Sylvia Andrew, but her marriage to Gowland, which produced a son named Peter, did not last and ended in 1918.

Gowland continued to work in small roles until he was aptly cast by von Stroheim in his masterpiece *Greed* as the gentle giant McTeague; a man driven to violence and murder after becoming obsessed with obtaining money. Sadly, most of Gowland's performance was edited away and lost because of von Stroheim's maniacal obsession with accuracy. In his attempt to remain true to the story, the director used Frank Norris' novel *McTeague* as part of the shooting script. Actual locations in the book were used in place of sets as von Stroheim attempted to make a visual copy of the story. Once completed, he presented Metro-Goldwyn-Mayer with an eight hour, forty two-reel film that infuriated the studio for its length and its investors for its cost. The movie was edited and re-edited until it had a running time of two and a half hours, which was still considered long but tolerable. Much of the excised film was burned for its silver content as a way to recoup some portion of its expected losses.

Gibson Gowland had appeared in a number of films and was usually cast as a villain, but in real life, he was a kindly, rugged individualist who marched to a different drumbeat. He eschewed the luxury associated with movie stars and instead purchased a small house near Malibu that had neither electricity nor plumbing and where he cooked using a kerosene stove. After his divorce, he allowed his ex-wife and her new husband to live in his home so that his son could have uninterrupted contact with his mother. He was even instrumental in getting the newlyweds to work on various films projects. Eventually, as can be expected, the situation became untenable and Gowland sought full custody of his son, which he won allowing visitation rights for his wife. Peter would join his father on the set of *Hell Harbor.*

Actor Jean Hersholt graduated from the Copenhagen Art School and made a living as a portrait painter in his native Denmark. Working as an artist and actor in stage plays, he became interested in the new medium of film and worked briefly for the Danish pioneering filmmaker Ole Olsen in the earliest days of the studio that would grow to become the Nordisk Film Kompagni; at the time, however, it was simply known as Ole Olsen's Film Factory. Hollywood lured Hersholt with its seemingly endless acting opportunities, offered in a nation that was beginning to dominate the industry. His chance to visit the United States presented itself in 1915 when as reported; he was offered a position to oversee the Danish National Art Exhibit at the San Francisco World's Fair. That same year he made his first appearance in an American film called *The Disciple;* a western directed by William S. Hart and written by Thomas Ince.

Once sound started making its feeble way into movies, Hersholt's star began to dim. Despite his exceptional acting abilities, the studio executives felt that his accent was too pronounced and the well of offers began to dry up. Henry King had worked with Hersholt in 1924 casting him as Ed Munn in his silent version of *Stella Dallas*. The two had become friends, and when he presented the scenario to United Artists, King told them that he wanted Hersholt for the part of Joseph Horngold. The executives scoffed at the idea, but King was determined. He took the script home and rewrote the part of the merchant, making him a foreigner on the island. At the next executive meeting, the director once again suggested Hersholt as the new character, and this time he obtained their approval. It is ironic that the actor, whom the studios found inadequate for sound, was later universally praised by the critics as the strongest performer in *Hell Harbor*.

From that moment, Hersholt continued to rise professionally; from bit parts to costar, to leading man. He would go on to master film and radio performances and eventually appeared on television in the final years of his life. He came to the desert film community around the same time as his off-screen friend and on-screen nemesis Gibson Gowland. Their careers would travel the same path; intersecting at a few points, but ultimately ending at different destinations.

Harry Radford Allen was born in Sydney, New South Wales, Australia in 1883. He had toured the Australian theater circuits and married a fellow performer, Marjorie Condon in 1910. By 1912, Allen had ended the marriage by leaving the country and setting sail for Vancouver, Canada. He would never write or make contact with his wife again.

In 1915 Marjorie was granted a divorce on the grounds of desertion.

Allen became employed with a touring company that performed *The Better 'Ole*, a British musical comedy based on a beloved English cartoon strip called *Old Bill* that chronicled the hapless exploits of a World War I soldier. He would also work in a number of Broadway plays including *For Goodness Sake*, featuring Fred and Adele Astaire at the Lyric Theater in 1922.

His role in *Hell Harbor* would be short and physically painful. As Peg Leg, he would be required to wear a tapered wooden leg that was secured to his knee while his real leg was bent and tied behind him. The prosthetic irritated Allen's knee, but like a real Vaudeville trouper, he did not complain. In the opening scene, he is photographed walking down the narrow wooden plank streets of the town.

Al St. John; an agile comic actor who was one of the original Keystone Cops and nephew of Roscoe "Fatty" Arbuckle would portray Wade's First Mate, Bunion. St. John was nearly unable to participate in the film due to legal issues with an ex-wife who was seeking $1,600.00 in back alimony. A judge in California who was not sympathetic to the actor sentenced him to an indefinite stay in the county jail until the back payments were satisfied. In a bold legal maneuver; St. John's attorney filed a writ of habeas corpus citing that the judge had overstepped his authority by sentencing his client to the open-ended term of confinement. St. John pleaded that he was "broke" and would be facing a life sentence if the order was allowed to stand. The court agreed and ordered his immediate release, thus allowing him to participate in the film.

By far the most popular and congenial member of the cast was Paul E. Burns; a blistering with pride first-generation Irish-American from Philadelphia. He arrived on the *Hell Harbor* set with a quick wit, and enough show business experience to fill ten amphitheaters. Burns would transform his character, Blinky into a Hibernian bard that was part poet and part roustabout. He would add moments of slapstick to lighten the mood. This gift is best demonstrated in one particular scene where he is supposed to kill Bob Wade.

Burns came from a family of stage entertainers, and at the tender age of four made his acting debut. At eighteen he traveled the Vaudeville circuit performing skits and absorbing as much information as he could. At nineteen, he left his employer and formed his own troupe. As the leader of an entertainment enterprise, he was responsible for all business arrangements including the hiring of performers. One actor that he had hired many years earlier was a young man named Henry King.

Twelve-year-old George Bookasta was born in Kansas City, Missouri of Syrian parents. The family moved to California where his father found work as an extra in movies. George was barely walking when he made an on-stage appearance at the Paramount Theater in Los Angeles dressed as Charlie Chaplin's character The Little Tramp. In the audience, that day was a patron so entertained by the young child that he ordered United Artists to sign the young man to a contract. Serendipitously, that patron was Chaplin himself.

At age six he was cast in his first film *Rosita;* starring Mary Pickford. He later made two more films without a screen credit for United Artists. Playing Spotty in *Hell Harbor* would prove to be one of the greatest roles of a career that continued through the nineteen thirties and forties but was relegated to bit parts.

8

ON September 8, 1929, Henry King returned to Tampa by rail and brought with him the sound equipment plus the entire cast minus Velez. She would arrive one week later to greater fanfare. The train arrived at Union Station about 5:30 that morning, but the travelers did not exit their cars until 7:15. Approximately five hundred excitedly curious residents came to greet the stars along with a delegation from the Chamber of Commerce. John Holland was the first to step onto the platform and into the Florida sunshine. He would be followed by Gibson Gowland, Gene Herscholt, Al St. John, Paul Burns, Harry Allen, and young George Bookasta. After a few speeches, handshakes, and photos; the stars were taken to the Floridan hotel. They would report to work the next day at 8:00 A.M. to begin filming. For the next 70 days, all involved would make Tampa their home on the fourth floor of the opulent hotel.

Along with the cast members came some of the production staff: Scriptwriter Clarke Silvernail, composer Eugene Berton, Max Larey who was in charge of script continuity, film editor Lloyd Nosler, photographer William Fraker, and cameraman and Mack Stengler. There was also an army of assistants and staff. Some of the stars and higher-ups brought their wives and immediate family. Gowland brought his son Peter.

Also on the train was a twenty-two-year-old ingénue

named Carlotta Monti. Born Carla Montijo in Los Angeles, California; she claimed to have been a former Miss Hollywood and found some work in films, usually without an onscreen credit. Her most notable role at the time was in the original 1925 version of *Ben-Hur* where she can be seen in one scene as a slave girl standing in the background. Monti was invited to work on *Hell Harbor* after completing the role of Juanita in the film, *In Old California* where Ernest Rovere had served as its sound engineer and Harry Allen had co-starred. When she was offered an opportunity to work with them again on *Hell Harbor*, she accepted and boarded the train to Tampa. Her career would remain one of small parts in low budget movies until a chance meeting in 1932 with W.C. Fields garnered for her an unexpected place in Hollywood history.

At the age of 25, Monti became the consort and confidante of the misanthropic comic who was more than twice her age. Her memoir; *W.C. Fields and Me,* memorializes the often turbulent, sometimes loving, yet ultimately tragic relationship that bound the two together for the last fourteen years of Field's life. In 1976, Academy Award winners Rod Steiger and Valerie Perrine were cast as the couple in a film adaptation of her book. Carlotta Monti makes her final movie appearance in the film, as yet again, an extra.

The popular Cuban band Sexteto Habanero arrived for duty a day earlier and would launch itself internationally through the film.

Casting Director Wellington Scott was brought on to hire the local acting talent. After examining the script and consulting with the director, it was decided that the extras should have a decidedly Spanish look. This was another departure from the book, where Rida Johnson Young described the island as a part of the British Empire; ruled by a viceroy, and populated by people who were culturally and hereditarily English.

Advertisements went out to the local community for extras before shooting commenced. The second floor of the Chamber of Commerce where the casting offices were located was packed with would be thespians. Notes and photographs of each aspirant were maintained in a "type file" by the production team. Wellington Scott would cast the male players, while his Cuban born assistant casting director, Rosita Gil was in charge of choosing the female extras. Beauty contests and open casting calls were also held at the various Spanish and Cuban clubs of Ybor City in association with the Chamber of Commerce. The first local hired was a recent graduate of Hillsborough High School named Hilda Lopez. Her picture had been submitted for consideration along with a few hundred others and she was personally selected by Scott prior to the arrival of Gil. According to the Tampa Morning Tribune; the pretty eighteen-year-old, with dark hair and coal black eyes, was chosen because she "was regarded as a perfect Spanish type."

Another interesting find by Wellington Scott was that of Kitty May Arnold. Miss Arnold attended Hillsborough High School in 1923 and upon graduation, moved to Hollywood with a recommendation from the Irish born film director Rex Ingram, whom she met during a visit to Miami. She appeared in a number of small parts in some large studio productions.

In *The Singing Fool*, she played opposite Al Jolson, but to her chagrin, she would find out at the film's premiere that her part had been completely edited out. She had come back to Tampa for a vacation, and out of sheer coincidence heard about the *Hell Harbor* production.

"High hopes, disappointments, thrills and sometimes a bit of a nightmare," was how she defined show business. While the striking blue-eyed redhead never quite reached the level of stardom to which she aspired, Kitty May Arnold could be credited as the first "scream queen" in the movies. Her talent is exhibited at the end of *In Old Arizona*, when the cheating lover of both the Cisco Kid and the sheriff that seeks to capture him, played by Dorothy Burgess, is killed; it is Arnold's scream that is used in the dubbing process.

Along with the beauty contests and the photo submissions, there were also recommendations made by others to the casting office. Fifty sailors were suggested by the Seaman's Institute; speakeasy bartenders, gamblers, and lawmen were all tapped as extras.

On September 12th, filming began for the long-awaited scene anticipated by the Tampa extras. In it, Harry Allen's character Peg Leg enters the El Marino Cafe and launches the dramatic beginning of the story. The tracking shots of the bar and its dancers have been beautifully photographed thanks to the camera work of Mack Stengler and John P. Fulton. Sound engineer Ernest Rovere overdubs some of the dialogue of the multilingual patrons in order to produce the effect of a boisterous place while Sexteto Habanero's music fills the room. Shots of the band dwell slowly on their exotic instruments

further confirming the authenticity of the locale. This is the
scene that introduces the fictional denizens of Hell Harbor,
portrayed by the real the people of Tampa. It is also arguably
the best scene in the film and a shining example of what King
had imagined when he took on the project.

The extras began work at 6:30 A.M. and were sent to
a huge makeup and wardrobe tent with a canvas wall in
the middle separating the sexes. The tent was overseen by
Rosita Gil and Richard Harland who advised and counseled
the nervous amateurs. Rehearsals did not begin until noon
and actual shooting began even later. September in Florida
can still be hot, and the day of the scheduled shooting was
no exception. Temperatures by noon were in the 80s. The
El Marino, which had very little ventilation, was sweltering.
The heat was made even more intense by the large 1000 watt
lights needed to illuminate the indoor shots. Henry King
instructed the extras to wait outside until they were absolutely needed for the scene. Once called inside, they took
their places. Suddenly, before ordering the cameras to start
rolling, the director shouted;

"Forget you are in Tampa."

Upon command, the extras dutifully performed; some
danced, some loitered, while others engaged in drunken
banter. Each action helped to transform the small Florida
movie set into a seedy Caribbean bar. For a few moments,
the extras were no longer cigar makers and typists —they
were movie stars, brightly shining and blissfully lost in a
cloud of dreams. A lucky few would be transformed into real
actors and actresses and propelled to the bigger, more lavish

soundstages of Hollywood. Others would go on to lead quiet lives with memories that echoed through the years.

Julia Ybañez divorced her husband Thomas in Jacksonville, Florida and moved to Tampa with her daughter Ruth to work as a secretary for Equitable Life. A well-respected woman in the community, she was asked by the city to serve as a hostess for the visiting movie personnel in the summer of 1929. Henry King graciously paid back the hospitality he received from her by offering a small part to seventeen-year-old Ruth once production began in September. Ruth, who had performed in local theater and had just been admitted to the Florida State College for Women, readily accepted when the offer eventually came.

Young Ruth appears in the first scene of the film, walking toward Peg Leg on a narrow sidewalk, where he gives her a wolf's whistle and she runs off. Although described in detail by the local newspaper reporters who witnessed it; her solo scene appears to have been cut in the final edit. It is interesting to note, however, that the only 35mm nitrate print of the film is missing six minutes, so her scene may have been included in the original theatrical release.

Her role as a poor island girl belied the fact that in real life she was related to Spanish literary nobility. Her uncle on her father's side was the noted author Vincente Belasco Ibañez, whose novels: *The Four Horseman of the Apocalypse* and *Blood and Sand* were made into blockbuster films in both the silent and sound eras. The original productions of each movie featured Rudolf Valentino in the lead roles, and it was *The Four Horsemen of the Apocalypse* that catapulted the young Italian dancer to stardom. Ruth's role in *Hell Harbor* was discussed in Hollywood and led to a contract with Paramount Studios.

After *Hell Harbor,* Ybañez would arrive in Hollywood with her mother and grandmother. They were met at the train station by Harry Ham, a friend who had been part of the production staff in Tampa and now worked for Paramount. Once the trio was ensconced in their hotel, Ruth was told that she could unpack later. Ham then drove her to the studio where she would immediately begin work on the set of *For the Defense;* sitting in a jury box and listening to William Powell plead his case to the court. Once settled in the movie capital, Ruth Ybañez would eventually adopt her mother's maiden name and work as Ruth Hall, co-starring opposite such stars as the Marx Brothers and John Wayne.

****

At the Tampa Morning Tribune newspaper, a thirty-five-year-old reporter named Rondo Hatton was given the enviable assignment of reporting on the day-to-day events of *Hell Harbor's* production. Hatton had been somewhat of a hometown legend in his youth; making headlines in the paper long before he wrote bylines for it. He was also the cousin of Sheriff Luther Hatton.

At Hillsborough High School's class of 1913, he was hailed as a champion football player and voted the best looking boy in his class. Upon graduation, the popular young man originally from Hagerstown, Maryland, would

continue his prowess on the gridiron at the University of
Florida. He then served in the U.S. Army Infantry as part of
the American Expeditionary Forces sent to France to fight in
the First World War and attained the rank of 2nd Lieutenant.

Hatton fought and was wounded in the Argonne
Offensive. It was while he was recuperating in an army
hospital for lung damage suffered in a mustard gas attack that
he began to exhibit symptoms inconsistent with a pulmonary
wound. Facial swelling and complaints of severe body ache
baffled the military doctors. It would later be determined that
he was experiencing the onset of Acromegaly: a rare disease
of the pituitary gland that secrets growth hormone into the
bloodstream, producing continued enlargements and ulti-
mate deformity of the soft tissues and bones of the face and
hands. It is generally caused by a noncancerous adenoma
tumor of the pituitary, but may also be brought about by
tumors in the lung, pancreas, or adrenal glands. Hatton
always claimed that the disease came from his exposure to
mustard gas, but Acromegaly usually appears later in life and
is only associated with tumors. Aside from the ever-growing
facial distortions; the condition also brings with it other
ailments like an enlarged, weakening heart and a permanent
swelling of the vocal cords which affect the tone of the voice.
Hatton was discharged from the army with a pension for his
wound and returned to Tampa, where he was hired on as the
sports editor of the Tribune.

While Rondo Hatton suffered physically, he also suffered
quietly in the awful solitude that only those with an affliction
can experience. He watched as his marriage dissolved, and he

saw the unwanted pity of those who knew him, and felt how they distanced themselves from him. He once wrote: "To any casualty, the hardest part of war is coming home."

The assignment to cover the film and its stars, however, changed Hatton's life. He would make lemonade out of a lemon and move forward into a new direction gradually gaining acceptance of his condition and even using it to his advantage. When Hatton arrived on the set, Director Henry King was struck by his unusual appearance and offered him a small role in the film; the role would be that of a bouncer in the El Marino Cafe. In his scene, dancers sway past him as Hatton stands in the middle of the dance floor smoking a cigarette and looking menacingly for any sign of trouble. He portrays a man who will accept no nonsense; a man who has seen much and has been scarred by it. Hatton, without saying a word, plays the role with an eerie clarity.

While a number of extras were offered contracts in Hollywood, one rejection of such an offer became a note-worthy story in the *Tampa Morning Tribune*. Nathan Gonzalez was a Florida born resident of Ybor City. His unique look, which featured a shaved head, landed him an early role in *Hell Harbor* where he is seen playing cards with Gowland in the El Marino and later throwing a chair at John Holland. His refusal of a career in Hollywood was simple: He loved Tampa and simply did not want to leave it. Despite the leadership of the city wanting to see the success of its own in the movie business, it must have delighted the Chamber of Commerce to hear that for some, the seductiveness of a California dream did not match the desirability of Tampa's real charms —a selling point for the future if there ever was one.

Rosita Gil arrived from California with Richard Harlan. The two were a couple that would eventually marry, and in true Hollywood style, end their relationship acrimoniously. For now, however, they would work on the film in their appointed capacities. Unofficially they would also serve as advisors on Latin American culture. Gil was a native of Cuba and Harland was an American born in Peru where his father worked for the U.S. Embassy. After the casting duties were completed Harlan and Gil departed for Cuba to buy props, and dresses for the female players.

In *Out of the Night,* Rida Johnson-Young imagined an island somewhere in the Antilles inhabited only by those whose ancestors were White English pirates. She described in the novel that the Black population of Abaco lived on a separate island nearby and that very little commerce occurred between the neighbors. Henry King and Casting Director Wellington Scott understood that the depiction of such a racially isolated place in the Caribbean was simply not a believable visual for the movie. So they announced that a large number of Black extras would be hired for the film.

Making and adhering to such a pronouncement created a series of challenges for the production in the segregated south of 1929. Assurances had to be made that the races would be kept apart socially to comply with the local Jim Crow ordinances and they could only be brought together when it was absolutely necessary for the purposes of their employment. Separate areas for dining and breaks, as well as pay windows, needed to be established to ensure that even the most casual or accidental intermingling did not take place.

At a time when certain scenes containing Black actors were excised from movies distributed in the south; Henry King, a Southerner himself, places the name of a Tampa African American extra named Ulysses Williams in the opening credits along with the featured players. Williams portrays Nemo; one of Bob Wade's crewmen and appears in a brief walk-on early in the film where he is watched by Blinky as he unloads a keg from the ship. He is later seen rushing into the El Marino Cafe to join in on the fight that has broken out. While Nemo does not have a speaking part, his fight scene ends with his killing of Rondo Hatton's character. At the movie's premiere in Tampa, the actions of Williams were roundly applauded by an audience that was swept up in the action despite the fact that such depictions of interracial violence were generally considered unacceptable.

Why King chose to list this extra in the opening credits is unclear. If the director simply wanted to give a courtesy screen credit to a local actor, then certainly Rondo Hatton's name would have had more recognition to the people of Tampa. There appears to be something more to the placing of Williams' name among the players. Perhaps this was King's way to note the contributions of the film's African American cast members who did not receive any meaningful coverage in the press releases or the newspapers of the day. Whatever the director's reason might have been, or whatever social statement he was attempting to make, the strong young

man, who never appeared in another film, would be indelibly linked to *Hell Harbor* as one of its stars.

9

LUPE Velez' arrival in Tampa at 9:00 A.M. on September 17, 1929, was greeted with all the pomp and ceremony of a visiting empress. The Governor of Florida, Doyle Carlton and his wife, Nell came from Tallahassee to personally meet the actress at the train station. Henry King and John Holland were also there, along with an entourage of sixteen young women who came as part of the welcoming committee; they were clad in bright traditional Spanish dresses, complete with mantillas and fans.

As she stepped out of Union Station's main entrance and into the city center, Velez first saw the glint of polished bayonets attached to rifles held high by members of the National Guard to form an arch under which she would walk. Velez would also behold a sea of well-wishers to welcome her: Men wearing straw brimmed hats, and women arrayed in the latest fashions of the day. After a few obligatory photos, the governor whisked her off in his car to the Floridan Hotel where a sold-out gala breakfast was being held in her honor organized by Trenton Collins of the Chamber of Commerce. Passing through the well polished revolving doors of the hotel, Lupe was greeted by the hotel's managerial staff and the serenade of mariachi music by members of the Orquestra Mexicana de Charros Mondragon. The Mexican group had just performed a sold out concert in Tampa a week earlier but stayed in town longer to help welcome their fellow compatriot in the spacious lobby of the Floridan.

Lupe was then escorted into the main dining room where three hundred people rose in applause as she entered. Speeches were made by the Master of Ceremony, Trenton Collins; The Chamber president Carl Brorien, and Mayor McKay's representative at the event, the Director of Public Works: R. Wallace Davis. Henry King spoke for everyone involved in the production when he praised and thanked Tampa for its support of the project. To underscore his feelings, King also read a congratulatory letter from Will Hayes, President of the Motion Picture Producers and Distributors Association recognizing Tampa and its importance in the making of a motion picture that was expanding the boundaries of how movies were made.

Lupe Velez also spoke as to how happy she was to be in Tampa, and how it was her first time being greeted by a governor. As if the outpouring of social generosity had not been enough for her, the actress was also awarded an honorary membership in the Tampa Business Women's Club. During the breakfast, Sexteto Habanero performed its repertoire of son Cubano music.

Afterwards, Lupe adjourned to suite 1714 which had a panoramic skyline view of the city she was about to conquer. She would rest for a few hours until the second part of Tampa's charm offensive would take place. The management of the Floridan considered her privacy and her comfort their mission. A latticework door and frame was constructed in the hallway to block any uninvited visitors from disturbing the star, and a Spanish speaking maid was assigned to her rooms at all times.

At two o'clock in the afternoon, Lupe Velez would once again find herself being chauffeured, this time to Plant Park on the grounds of the Tampa Bay Hotel. The building was once the jewel of Tampa with its distinctive minaret topped roof. It was built in 1888 by railroad baron Henry B. Plant and sat on over 100 acres. The hotel served as a self-contained resort that catered to royalty, captains of industry, and various celebrities of the day. Colonel Teddy Roosevelt and his military staff occupied it before embarking to Cuba during the Spanish American War, and Babe Ruth signed his first Major League baseball contract within its walls. However, by 1929, its glory days were finished and the hotel found itself replaced by more modern structures. In a few years, it would close but later be reopened with a new purpose as the University of Tampa.

The festivities at the park for Lupe were personally organized by Chamber of Commerce President Carl Brorien, and no degree of failure was allowed. Even the timing of the event was set for 2:30 P.M. to avoid the seasonal late afternoon rains.

As she was walked onto the outdoor stage wearing a green dress; a band played both The Star Spangled Banner and the Mexican national anthem. There were more speeches made by the politicians and the presenters despite the humid heat and the hot Florida sun. Mayor McKay, who was unable to attend the breakfast, presented Velez with the keys to the city while a sea of five thousand adoring fans —a full five percent of Tampa's population— looked on in wonder.

By coming a week after the rest of the cast, all the attention which was to be shared with them was instead solely lavished upon the film's leading lady. If her late arrival was a publicity stunt it surely worked.

A few nights later, Velez would walk a few steps from her hotel and perform at the Tampa Theater. The ornate movie house had been showing Henry King's *She Goes to War* as a way to introduce the local population to the director's work and some of the actors who were in town.

The film tells the story of a young society woman, played by Eleanor Boardman, who disguises herself as her fiancé in order to take his place on the battlefield during the First World War. The film also featured John Holland and Al St. John who were also in attendance that evening, but it was Lupe that the audience came to see. On the baroque stage of the theater, the actress entertained the crowd by performing some comedy routines and impressions. She did not disappoint her audience. The moviegoers that night were also unknowingly one of the last to see *She Goes to War* in its original form. In 1939 the film would be drastically edited and used as a tool to promote the isolationist cause against U.S. involvement in the World War II. No known copy of the original exists.

10

THE public beach at Rocky Point had been closed to anyone that was not part of the construction crew on Labor Day of that year. The anger that was expressed by the few who planned to spend a day relaxing on the white sandy shore was soon forgotten once filming began. For Tampans; their city had become a place where movie stars could be seen and locals could be discovered. Virtually everyone knew someone affiliated with the picture and people looked closer at their surroundings in hopes of seeing Lupe Velez on one of her massive shopping sprees or John Holland taking a stroll. The city went mad with Hell Harbor fever and the production became the main topic of conversation at lunch counters, barbershops, office buildings. Any place where two people might gather the subject of *Hell Harbor* would most assuredly arise, and wherever there was just one solitary person, it was likely that he or she was pondering the subject.

The city that was sometimes considered a little provincial found itself fortified, full of pride and ready for a ride that would put it on par with the glamorous movie capitals of the world. Imagination became belief for everyone in Tampa as film executives constantly extolled the virtues of the area. Emil Jansen, who was Vice President of United Artists Corporation and in charge of distribution of its films, had already, pre-booked *Hell Harbor* into every major theater in the southern United States. A film shot completely on location was more than a novelty; it was a new wave in cinema, and it would most assuredly continue. Interest in exhibiting the film in other parts of the country was growing and the tropical locale would be a selling point in the northern states, particularly in the winter. Jansen himself often vacationed in Florida and decided to stay for some of the filming.

"Tampa will get volumes of publicity from our promotion campaign," Jansen commented in an interview. "Hundreds of news articles will be published concerning the location and its beauty. These will be read by other producers of the industry and I am sure Tampa stands an excellent chance of getting additional motion picture productions on the strength of the glowing descriptions our organization will broadcast concerning our Rocky Point location."

United Artists was planning to cross-market the film through radio advertisements, newspaper stories, and articles in trade publications. It would also publish sheet and phonograph music from the soundtrack. Tampa saw an unimaginably bright future taking shape.

11

SOUND becomes another star in *Hell Harbor*, where nuances become pronouncements under the direction of Henry King and his audio engineer, Ernest Rovere, using the RCA Photophone System. In the opening scene, Harry Allen's character, Peg Leg can be heard walking; each step of his wooden leg can be heard striking the wooden street planks as he rushes to sell pearls to Horngold. The squeaky shoes of Horngold are heard behind the door of his closed shop, even before the audience sees him, as he eventually answers the vigorous knocking by the anxious pearl seller.

The actors were specifically chosen for, or encouraged to speak their lines with unique accents: Spanish for Velez, British for English born Gowland and Australian Harry Allen. Danish born Herscholt would affect an Eastern European inflection for his lines, while Paul Burns of Philadelphia plays Blinky with an Irish brogue.

Music is another important element in the film. In the quest to create a realistic Caribbean tone to *Hell Harbor*, the production brought the popular Son Cubano band Sexteto Habanero to Tampa from Cuba to supply most of the soundtrack.

In the late 1920s, Latin American music was finding its way onto the dance floors of the United States and Europe, and the rhythms of a musical style called "Son" was Cuba's best kept- secret. Son was a mixture of Spanish guitars and

African percussions. Its origins trace to the island's eastern-most providence, Oriente where African descendants added bongo drums and the marimbula to the guitars and songs of the Spanish population. Over the years son moved across the country and adopted other regional sounds. While popular, it was considered a provincial form of musical expression and was even banned in some public places until Cuban president Gerardo Machado invited the band Tuna Liberal, to perform at his 54th birthday party in 1925.

One of the island's most popular son bands was Sexteto Habanero. Originally founded in 1916 and called Cuarteto Oriental as a homage to their home providence of Oriente, Cuba. The band recorded for U.S. based Columbia Records as early as 1917. Over the years, two more musicians were added and by 1925 they were known as Sexteto Habanero.

The band's arrival in Tampa would be a historic one. Aside from the original founding members; Felipe Neri Cabrera, Guillermo Castillo, Carlos Godinez, and Gerardo Martinez, the onscreen players would also include Andres Sotolongo, and Miguelito Garcia. A trumpet player named Jose Iterian was later added to the ensemble, and though his presence created the formation of a septet, his addition did not lead to a change in the name of the group. Their performance would be the first visual record of a Son Cubano band at work. Henry King did not hide or disregard their talent; he placed them front and center as part of the action in the El Marino Cafe. Son Cubano had arrived; it would no longer be hidden in the backwoods and private parties of Oriente

Providence: it would now be seen and heard by millions, growing and evolving into what is referred to today as Salsa.

If Son Cubano had put a dance in the step of the music lover, then Cuban composer Ernesto Lecuona had engraved a song on its heart. As the opening credits of *Hell Harbor* roll, his composition *Noche Azul* becomes the movie's theme song, uniquely performed by Sexteto Habanero. This interpretation of the song was not recorded anywhere else, so it is only through the film that this version can be heard.

Ernesto Lecuona was a Cuban musical patriot who absorbed the Spanish, indigenous, and African musical heritage of his country to create melodies that transformed them into symphonic harmonies. His work became a source of national pride and almost led to an international dispute when he died at age 68.

Lecuona's early life was a happy cacophony of music, Cuban nationalism, and Spanish culture. His father was a journalist born in the Spanish Canary Islands who immigrated to Matanzas and edited a newspaper. His mother, on the other hand, was a fervent Cuban nationalist who would raise money for the rebels seeking independence and fly the national standard whenever her husband's Spanish friends came to visit.

The Lecuona's had seven children who were all classically trained as musicians, but it was young Ernesto who was recognized as a prodigy at age eleven. His body of work would include *Grenada;* a musical paean that borrows Moorish cadences that at once bemoans the memory of the city's past while also praising its eternalness. *Maria La O* which tells the story of a broken-hearted Cuban girl using island rhythms to evoke her sadness, and *Always in My Heart;* a song he wrote for a Hollywood film of the same name in 1942 that was nominated for a Best Original Song Oscar but lost to *White Christmas.* The composer Maurice Ravel once remarked that Lecuona's "*Malagueña* is more beautiful and melodic than my *Bolero.*" Despite such recognition, his name is misspelled in the opening credits of *Hell Harbor:* It appears as Ernesto Lecvona.

Finding the communist regime of Fidel Castro repugnant to his strong religious and personal beliefs, he left Cuba in 1960 and for a short time lived in Tampa before moving on to New York. In 1963 he traveled to the Canary Islands on a vacation and died of complications from asthma. The Cuban government requested that his remains be repatriated to the island, but the regional government of Malaga, Spain sought to have their adopted son interred in the cemetery there. He was eventually buried in the Gate of Heaven Cemetery in Westchester County, New York. At the time of his death, he had one stipulation: To be reinterred in Cuba, the land of his inspiration, once the island was again free.

A former child Vaudeville star turned classically trained composer named Gene Berton was brought into the production to supply a theme song as well as additional music and lyrics. King actually wanted music kept to a minimum because it tended to drown out the dialogue, but he did include it where it could be highlighted or when it was vital to the scene.

Viewers are introduced to Lupe Velez' character, Anita

during an evening get together on the beach with her friends Blinky, a one-eyed Irish beachcomber and Spotty, the young boy who has a crush on her. Blinky accompanies Anita on his accordion while she sings with great vigor, the song *Coconito* by Mexican composer Lorenzo Barcelata who, unfortunately, is not mentioned in the credits. The inclusion of this song into the picture was made at the request of Velez herself and allowed King to showcase the singing talents of the actress and further underscore the power of the medium.

At some point, however, it became apparent that an important element to the story was missing. Namely, that there was no connection between the pirate Captain Morgan and Anita in the screenplay. The progenitorial relationship that had been an integral part of the novel was conspicuously missing. To fill this gap, Clark Silvernail added additional dialogue to the beach scene where Anita asks Blinky to sing a song about her ancestor. Gene Berton was asked to compose the piece which in the end results in an annoyingly long sea shanty that prattles on about the cruelty of Morgan. Remarkably, King considered this one of the highlights of the film. In his judgment: Blinky was an admirer of Morgan so his song should represent the relationship between the singer and the subject rather than the pirate and his descendant. The director, by maintaining this belief, incorrectly transfers the importance of Morgan's place in the story away from the main character, which is defined by the relationship, to a minor character that has been written into the script.

The theme song of the film was slated to be *Caribbean Love Song*. Berton wrote the piece within an hour of reading the script: A feat that very much impressed King. Berton traveled to Tampa with the idea of assembling a chorus of sixty to seventy-five voices to perform the song. King, however, had a more visually grandiose concept about how the song would be introduced. He imagined Holland and Velez staring starry-eyed at each other onboard the schooner as the Mexican singer Raoul Mondragon drifted past them performing the song while standing in a skiff accompanied by a beautiful girl strumming a guitar. The logistics of shooting this scene would prove to be too difficult and in the end, King would decide to use a son version of *Caribbean Love Song* for the scene. The skiff, however, would be docked while a guitarist from Sexteto Habanera played the tune and a vocalist performed it in Spanish. During the song, Anita is seen standing in a rowboat; the wind in her hair and Rocky Point behind her as Blinky and Spotty paddle her out to Bob Wade's schooner.

The director later decided to use Lecuona's *Noche Azul* as the opening song. Berton's music would be used as a background piece for the love scene instead. The placement of *Caribbean Love Song* as part of the film's action, as opposed to it being played over the initial credits not only enhances the piece but also the scene for which it is played. It sets the tone for the two lovers as they surrender their hearts and ultimately their futures to each other aboard Bob Wade's ship.

12

THE technical difficulties of filming an all talking film on location were new and unforeseen. Sound equipment was big and bulky. Microphones had to be close enough to pick up the actors voices, but far enough as not to be in the camera's view. Precautions had to be taken for exterior shots against the wind, screeching seagulls, and rustling branches. Additional electrical lines had to be run onto Rocky Point from the nearest utility poles that were nearly one mile away. The 1000 amperes supplied by each line would be enhanced by an additional generator to provide more power to the lamps.

Shooting on board a schooner was even more difficult. Electrical lines had to be stretched from land, over the water, resting at intervals on smaller boats to stay dry. Cameras needed to be set up and taken down on the narrow walkways of the Elsie and balanced to prevent unwanted movement under the rippling waves.

The hot sun also affected lighting at times. One of the early scenes in the motion picture, where the character of Peg Leg walks to the El Marino at night was actually filmed during the day with large tarps to block out the sun; artificial lighting was then used to give the appearance of moonlight.

Cameramen Mack Stengler and John P. Fulton were the best in their field. Stengler had been working as a cameraman since the mid-1920s and had gained a reputation for quality photography; *Hell Harbor,* however, was to be his first sound film. While Stengler understood the art of cinematography, he was slightly reticent to work with sound on such a grand scale. He could see that the industry was changing and accepted the opportunity that Henry King had placed before him as a chance to learn and advance in his craft.

John P. Fulton was the maverick. Despite having less experience as a cameraman than Stengler, he had worked with sound and developed a niche in shooting special effects. King needed someone like him for the fight scene at the end of the movie, which exhibited more stunts and a higher level of violence than previously seen onscreen.

The sound equipment was cumbersome and arrived in two railroad freight cars. The R.C.A. Photophone system was the most advanced form of recording on the market. It used the Variable Area Method of optical sound recording. With this process, microphones are placed on the set and connected to the sound booth. Two cameras are used: one for the physical images on the set, and one for the sound images in the booth. A mechanism was locked into place to guarantee full synchronization of the images. As the sound comes through the microphones it passes through a galvanometer with a mirror so small it cannot be seen with the naked eye and creates a path of light carrying the recorded sounds via a beam that is then transferred onto the film. Later, the image only film and the sound film are coordinated and developed into a single positive to be run through a selenium cell converting the light impulses into sound on the frame.

The sound booth itself was a cramped, stainless steel

box that could hold a maximum of three people at a time. Acoustically made to block sounds from the outside, it was the most restrictive place on the set and only a select few were admitted into it. The elite club consisted of Ernest Rovere; Maintenance Engineer, Lin Rhodes; Power Engineer, Bert Cross; Sound Technician, Barney Summars, and Assistant Sound Engineer, Cliff Howard. Local Tampan, Bill Sullivan was hired to work as the Signal Man. His job was to be on the set and flip a switch on a control board to notify those working in the booth that Director King had begun filming. Despite its size and weight the booth was portable, with its own set of wheels for short moves on the set, or it could be mounted onto a truck for traveling greater distances.

To facilitate the better visuals, Barney Summars designed and built a revolving camera booth capable of following the actors while blocking out the distracting noises of the equipment. To be assigned this job was a form of torture. The operator (usually Fulton or Stengler) was placed into a poorly ventilated, cylindrical structure and could only communicate with the outside by a telephone attached to a speaker at the top of the turret. Every six minutes the door had to be opened to allow fresh air to enter the chamber, and to see if the man inside was all right. The hot, humid Florida climate turned this mechanism into a steam bath from which there was no recourse.

The best example of this device's use is exemplified in the opening shots of the film. The camera pans the tops of the island's palm trees, then focuses downward to follow Peg Leg walking down the street to Horngold's shop.

An elaborate field telephone system was installed on Rock Point so that Henry King could stay in touch with the cast and crew who were scattered throughout the island. When completed, there would be two master stations, a dozen field stations, and even a main switchboard operator.

Rocky Point had been brought into the future.

13

O N September 22, 1929, Father Mariano Gutierrez-Lanza, SJ, a Spanish born Jesuit priest and Director of the Belen Observatory in Havana, reported that a major hurricane was heading toward Andros Island in the Bahamas. His predictions were dire; the storm contained wind speeds of between 111-178 MPH, which under modern measurements would be considered a Category 3. He further warned that the path of the storm posed a direct hit to South Florida and advised a state of emergency preparedness for the area.

The east coast of Florida was worried but ready. A year earlier, the Okeechobee Hurricane killed over 2,500 people; made thousands more homeless, and decimated agriculture. While the authorities could not stop the force of nature that was speeding toward them, it could try to mitigate its effects. An order of evacuation was put in place for the Everglades and the surrounding areas. Trucks and trains transported evacuees as far west as Tampa and Fort Myers free of charge. The Red Cross was mobilized and shelters were set up for those who could not leave their homes.

Fr. Gutierrez-Lanza; a Georgetown educated meteorologist and astronomer proved to be correct. When the hurricane hit Florida's southernmost point just above the keys, it did so with wind speeds of 155MPH, the storm then took a northwest trajectory into the Gulf of Mexico. Damage in Florida was minimal, although the Miami-Fort Lauderdale area was affected by three tornados that the weather system brought with it.

Hurricanes are unpredictable and can change course at any time, but weather patterns surrounding them can also be devastating; delivering heavy rains and winds miles from the storm's eye. As the tempest that would become known as the Great Andros Island Hurricane of 1929 entered into the Gulf of Mexico and headed north, the city of Tampa kept a close eye on its movement.

On September 30th, the weather at Rocky Point was beautiful and mild; white, puffy clouds floated in a clear azure sky that created an environment conducive to filming. It was the typical calm before the storm and Henry King used the natural serenity to speed up his production schedule. The threat of the hurricane, however, was taken very seriously and the director ordered the set secured nearly a week earlier upon hearing of the storm's possible approach and intensity. A team headed by property manager Irving Melliken, was put together to preserve the set. Architect Haas was put in charge of protecting the structures, while Captain M.R. Dawley secured the ships in the harbor. Ernest Rovere had the job of safeguarding the sound equipment, and second assistant director Robert Brandt took charge of the props. A network of tarps, sandbags, and tie downs was being employed while Henry King and the actors continued to rehearse and shoot scenes.

Later that afternoon, a messenger came with the final warning that the storm was fast approaching. The production stopped and the remainder of the lights and sound equipment were taken down; leaving everyone hoping for the best. Five workers remained on Rocky Point throughout the storm to tend to the boats.

At 10:30 that evening harbor patrolman Steve Kissenger went to the Floridan and reported that the castle tower was in grave danger. A team of four was assembled; made up of Haas, Milliken, Harry Ham, and Kissenger. They sped out to Rocky Point and made it onto the island through rising waters. The power had been cut off and the island was immersed in darkness. Through the torrential rain, Haas could see that the direction of the wind was hitting the tower at full force and the bottom was eroding, which was the real danger. Five thousand sandbags, each weighing two hundred pounds, were protecting the other structures, but now they needed to be moved to the base of the castle immediately. During the inspection, the road leading to the island became completely submerged by the rising tide and became impassible. No additional help would be coming, so the nine men on the island went to work loading a small car with the sandbags at one end of the set and driving to the other. The rain beat down on them like bullets in different directions depending on the wind gusts. Some of the men that had to jump into the rough waters of the bay to put down the sandbags would be knocked down and covered by crashing waves. Once the task had been completed, everyone took refuge in one of the dark structures Haas had built, along with a number of huge rats. By 3:00 A.M. the water had receded enough to return to the Floridan.

Many stories have been told about the hurricane: most of

which tell of how the site was secured at the last minute, and then miraculously survived an onslaught of biblical proportions. The facts are: The movie crew had ample warning and was prepared. The hurricane was also far off in the Gulf of Mexico and dissipating in the cooler waters as it headed north. By the time the storm reached landfall again in the Florida Panhandle, it had weakened into a tropical storm. The movie set was never directly hit by the eye of the hurricane, only by its outer bands which also carried with them violent winds and heavy rains; the veracity of which was equally matched by the tenacity of the movie crew's preservation efforts.

The next day greeted Henry King with another placid day as he inspected the set and found minimal damage. As the tide rose, sandbags protected the interiors from flooding, and while there was some exterior beach erosion around the buildings, the village remained intact. The castle too stood undamaged. In the end, the greatest contributors to saving the production were Robert Haas and his construction crew. His placement of strong roofs on the buildings protected the interiors from a deluge from above, just as the sandbags had protected flooding from the ground level. The sturdiness of his walls had withstood the strong winds. In the early days of silent films, many "interior" shots were sets built without ceilings to allow for natural light. The acoustic demands of a sound picture, however, especially in a tropical location where the rustling of the palm trees could drown out the dialogue, required closed sets. Haas' knowledge of his craft is evident in the authenticity and architectural strength of his buildings; his commitment to the film is indisputable by his actions on the night of the storm.

The fleet of boats fared less well and most were tossed upon the land. The Elsie, which had been anchored in the harbor, was dragged toward the shore and significant damage was done to the hull of the schooner. It was returned to the water but would eventually sink.

Henry King would later comment that the worst part of the ordeal was his inability to capture the sound of the storm for the film. The expensive Photophone equipment had been taken inland and out of harm's way. It is interesting to consider, however, how the film may have been changed with the addition of a recorded storm. A hurricane plays an important role in the novel and it sets the heroine's story on a different course. The proposition of an added storm in the film might have broadened Henry King's vision for the movie. The inclusion of howling winds and torrential rain coupled with music, dialogue, and sound effects most certainly would have been a first in cinema. King, Rovere, Fulton, and Stengler however, understood that placing cameras and sound equipment into such inclement weather conditions was a suicide pact that would put the entire production at risk.

14

FILMING began promptly at 8:00 AM the morning after the storm and would continue without any major interruptions for another fifty days. During that time, the newspapers continued to follow each day of production and report on the activity taking place on Rocky Point.

Tampa became a city both envied and admired by other star-struck politicians throughout Florida; becoming for them, a place of pilgrimage and wonder. Just as Governor Carlton had traveled down from Tallahassee to personally greet Lupe Velez when she arrived that October, C.H. Reeder, Miami's Mayor also visited Tampa. Accompanying him was the City Treasurer of Jacksonville, Alexander Ray, and one Mr. E.P. Owens who held the title: Secretary of the Florida League of Municipalities. Officially, they came as civic leaders offering well wishes to Henry King and the production. Unofficially they came to bask in the glow of movie stars and tout their own cities attributes for future projects.

Lavish parties were held in the homes of Tampa's wealthiest residents to honor the actors and Henry King. The small Danish community of Tampa held a traditional "koffee klatch" in honor of Jean Hersholt at its Valhalla Lodge located on Franklin Street. Speeches welcoming the actor were given in Danish and English, and afterward, Hersholt spoke informally to his fellow Danes in a room festooned in the red and white colors of Denmark.

John Holland attended the release of his most recent movie, *Black Magic,* and gave an impassioned speech on the importance of supporting an airport in Tampa.

On the evening of September 23rd, the El Marino Cafe on the *Hell Harbor* set became the stage for one of the more comical parties thrown by the cast. It was given to celebrate the birthday of Ruth Collins, the wife of Trenton Collins. The theme of the evening was Nursery Night which required the stars to dress as babies and purchase gifts from the five and ten cent store. The villainous visage of Gibson Gowland delighted everyone as he entered the festivities clad in a long nightgown and baby bonnet.

As Tampa's daily life began to revolve more and more around the making of the movie, its collective psyche began to incorporate the film into its own culture. One of the city's most important social events was the Legionnaires Ball that was presented annually by the U.S.S. Tampa Post of the American Legion. The soirée was held to benefit Hillsborough County's disabled and unemployed veterans of WW I. The Ball's usual venue was the Davis Island Coliseum; a fortress-like, art deco structure built a few years earlier so that it could accommodate a large number of attendees for various events. The success of the 1929 Ball was particularly important because earlier that year, the Legion's fund for charitable works was lost in the failure of the bank where it was deposited.

The organizers of the event decided that *Hell Harbor*

would be the theme of the Ball. The planners would include a masquerade and a beauty contest made up of candidates from other legion chapters throughout Florida. Two other contests would take place: one for girls sponsored by Tampa area businesses, and a free for all open to any girl wishing to participate. The winners would each win an audition for a small part in the film and perhaps an opportunity at stardom.

As an active member of the Legion, Rondo Hatton was more than instrumental in convincing Henry King, the cast and crew to attend. Lupe Velez immediately accepted the invitation; stating that she felt an affinity for the American veterans because her own father had been a soldier in the Mexican Revolution. To further enhance ticket sales, she agreed to a dance with one lucky ticket holder who would be chosen by a special raffle the night of the Ball.

Writer Clarke Silvernail, who had served in the Hospital Corps in during the war, agreed to lend his support to a cause that was near to him even though he was still recovering from the illness that kept him confined to a bed during his train trip to Tampa. The disease was erroneously reported as malarial fever. In the end, the entire cast, production team, and United Artists film executives working in Tampa agreed, without reservation, to be a part of what they viewed as a noble cause. The affair would mark the only time that all levels associated with the film would gather together socially.

The opportunity to rub elbows with real movie stars and the possibility to win a dance with Lupe Velez sent ticket sales, priced at one dollar, soaring. The initial number of tickets sold out quickly and required an additional batch to be printed. Two hundred private tables were sold and Commander J. Frank Carmack, of the U.S.S. Tampa Legion, received notification that representatives from other area posts, including Bradenton to the south, Orlando to the east, and all the posts in Pinellas County would be in attendance with entrants in the beauty contests.

While the main ballroom would have the Sanchez Orchestra playing popular dance tunes, four side loges would be converted into a replica of the El Marino with Rondo Hatton reprising his role as manager and Sextetto Habanero providing the music. A bar was set up along one wall with bottles of various colored liquids, backlit to highlight their contents. Officially Prohibition was the law of the land, so no liquor was served. In reality, however, Tampa was as wet as the Gulf of Mexico, and many would arrive with a flask containing the beverage of their choice. The party was also being held on the night before the big University of Florida – VMI football game which promised to bring a much younger and celebratory crowd to the Ball.

Adding to the pandemonium was the masquerade element of the event. Local stores advertised sales on pirate attire as well as "Spanish Man and Spanish Woman" outfits. Because of the limited supply of costumes available in Tampa; the legion post, seeing yet another opportunity to raise money, opened a store downtown with 2000 costumes for purchase. Advertising for the Friday, October 4th event was everywhere and final preparations went on up until the last minute.

*****

On the night of the Ball, emergency vehicles raced to the Coliseum at the same time that the partygoers were starting to arrive. Traffic to the event was delayed for more than thirty minutes as firefighters and their equipment prevented cars from approaching the venue. A small fire had broken out at about 7:30 P.M. and was attributed to faulty wiring. While the damage was minimal and did not affect the festivities in any way; it is safe to assume that the butterflies of excitement fluttering in the stomachs of the organizers turned, for a brief time, into flying bats with no direction.

Once the Ball got underway, the guests socialized and danced. Costumed knights in homemade armor along with pirates, sailors, and spear-wielding savages cavorted with damsels, she-devils, and señoritas on the dance floor. The revelers kept their eyes on the doors whenever possible in order to be the first to see the movie stars when they arrived. As the night wore on nearly 5,000 people packed the building.

It was almost 10:00 P.M. when the stars made their entrance. Henry King, the cast, and members of the production were brought to their loges. All the actors were there including young George Bookasta. Then, as trumpets blared, Lupe Velez made her entrance separately. The explosive reaction of the crowd, which was beginning to resemble a boisterous mob, made it clear who they had come to see. It was estimated that one thousand people stood before her loge; yelling her name and clapping. After a special performance of Flamenco and Spanish dancing by students of a local dance school; the Master of Ceremonies asked director

King and his stars to come onto the stage, allowing Henry King to introduce his players.

A replica of the Peacock Throne was brought on stage for Lupe, and once she was seated in it, a surprise coronation ceremony began. A silver scepter was placed in her hand and a dazzling crown was placed upon her head; the same crown that was bestowed on the Queen of the local Gasparilla Festival. Her court consisted of selected ladies from Tampa society; themselves costumed and bejeweled. During the coronation, Henry King spoke privately to the M.C. and advised him that Lupe would not be taking part in the dance raffle. The director felt that the size and disposition of the crowd displayed an unsafe environment for the actress. The M.C. embarrassingly agreed and, to the disappointment of many, it was announced that the raffle and dance would not take place.

The beauty contests started immediately after the announcement in order to keep the evening's action moving and distracting the crowd from the negative news. Miss Marie Hlavaty of Sarasota won the competition of representatives from the visiting legion posts. Elizabeth Lott took the prize for the commercial division, and Ruby Jones won the free-for-all competition.

The festivities continued on until 3:00 A.M., and the U.S.S Tampa Post of the American Legion reported a windfall profit of $3,500 to fund its support of disabled and unemployed veterans.

*****

A few weeks later the Lions Club hosted a black-tie dinner at the Forest Hills Country Club for the cast and crew as a way to say thank you for choosing Tampa. Henry King and his brother were in attendance as were most of the actors except Lupe Velez. Local rising star, Ruth Ibanez came and was described as "stunning" by the local papers, while Count d'Esco's presence added European elegance to the affair. Each table had at least one member of the production sitting with the ticket holders.

As the night wore on, some of the invited guests decided to show their talents. Gene Berton sang *Caribbean Love Song;* Al St. John demonstrated how to do a pratfall without hurting himself, and George Bookasta performed a dance. The star of the evening, however, was Paul Burns. He performed a monologue he had written that portrayed a guest of honor making an after-dinner speech. Delivering his soliloquy with impeccable timing and facial expressions, Burns sent the room into frenzied bouts of laughter, and made it a memorable evening for all.

15

A S the production started to wind down, the cast members began to consider other opportunities. Jean Hersholt was signed to star in *Mamba,* the first film ever to be shot in Technicolor.

Lupe Velez was slated to play, the Spanish born wife of wandering Irish bard Antoine Raferty, in an adaptation of Donn Byrne's novel: *Blind Raferty and his Wife Hilaria.* The project was later abandoned by United Artists.

John Holland planned to return home to Greensboro, North Carolina for a respite, and the other cast members would head back to California once their services were no longer needed.

In an interview with the Tampa Sunday Tribune, Gibson Gowland announced that after completing *Hell Harbor* he would retire from movies and move to South Africa with his son, Peter. The day for which he had been saving was finally here; the day when he could say goodbye to Hollywood and its disingenuous ideals and return to the rugged, honest life "where a handclasp is genuine". After *Greed,* Gowland had shied away from the celebrity parties where contacts were made and jobs were found; choosing instead, to spend evenings with his son. He would take work in smaller roles; putting a little money aside from each film to finance the move. Now, with the completion of *Hell Harbor,* the final stack in the bankroll had been provided.

That was, at least, the plan as of September 22, 1929. Shortly after the interview, Gowland became acquainted with a twenty-year-old aspiring actress who was visiting the movie set named Rachelle Dervaes. Despite an age difference of over 30 years, the two were romantically attracted to one another and Gowland was instrumental in getting the pretty Tampa native a contract with Universal Pictures. She would eventually move to Hollywood, and he would rethink his plans about Africa and his career.

In 1933 Arthur and Rachel Dervaes of Tampa announced the engagement of their daughter Rachelle to Gibson Gowland. Gowland was working on the joint U.S. - German co-productions of *S.O.S Iceberg* in Greenland, plus a comedy made primarily for German audiences titled *North Pole, Ahoy!* The two had planned to marry in Switzerland, but once united, they decided to instead marry in England. Their ceremony was performed that same year at the Church of St. George, Hanover Square, London. In 1935, their son George was born.

In *S.O.S Iceberg*, Gowland plays an American named John Dragan who is part of a search party looking for a lost explorer in the Arctic. As was customary, two versions of the film were shot simultaneously; one in German for German moviegoers, and one in English for the American market. The female lead in the movie is Leni Riefenstahl who in a few years would become Nazi Germany's leading film director. It would take 18 months to film all of the movies.

S.O.S. Iceberg was part of the Natural Film Movement which was popular with German audiences at the time.

The stories were usually centered on the horrible beauty of nature and how the characters overcame its deadlier aspects. In *S.O.S Iceberg*, humans are stranded with polar bears on a diminishing mass of ice.

After completing the films for Universal Pictures and its German counterpart, Gowland returned to England. He and his new wife would live in London where Gowland had signed contracts with other British production companies.

Henry King was seeking other projects which would allow him to use the Tampa set again. He had made a comment to that effect in a newspaper interview and suddenly found himself inundated with every type of scenario imaginable from every part of Florida. Writers from Inspiration Pictures and United Artists, however, sent for his consideration, the most feasible idea: A film based on the play *Great Music* by Martin Brown.

Great Music had originally run at the Earl Carroll Theatre on Broadway a few years earlier and tells a story completely different than that of the scenario presented to King. The original play concerns a young composer who struggles but cannot find inspiration. He discovers that he has leprosy and begins to write his greatest work after being sent to a Marquesas Island colony.

The movie version deals with a musician who suffers amnesia when he is shipwrecked and is discovered by the inhabitants of a South Sea island. He falls in love with one of the native girls and lives a life of relative bliss until he begins composing a musical piece on an old piano found in an even older bar. With his memory gradually returning he suddenly realizes that he has a wife back home and is forced to find his way back; leaving the Island and the girl behind.

For King, the Hell Harbor set was perfect. The El Marino only needed a piano and the movie could be made quickly and inexpensively. He estimated that he could begin production in the spring.

While the people of Florida were inspired to write and submit scenarios to King; Tampan Leopoldo Gonzalez was inspired to compose a one-act Spanish language musical revue titled *La Pelicula de Rocky Point* (The Rocky Point Movie).

Gonzalez was born in the northern Spanish region of Asturias and arrived in Tampa by way of Cuba; where he worked as a Lector in the cigar factories of Ybor City. The role of the Lector was an esteemed one in the community. These were educated men hired by the factories or in some cases by the employees themselves to read aloud newspapers and great works of literature to the cigar makers as they worked. Good Lectors were also actors; using different voices to bring life to the characters when reading a book by Flaubert or Tolstoy.

Leopoldo Gonzalez was a triple threat. Along with being a Lector, he was the editor of the newspaper, La Prensa in Ybor City, and had written, as well as directed, a number of plays for the local Spanish language theater companies. He also composed music, and published poetry. Politically active locally and a strong supporter of Mayor McKay, Gonzalez also gained a degree of fame beyond Tampa when he recorded a popular Paso Doble called *No Pasaran* in support of the Republican Loyalists during the 1936 - 1939 Spanish Civil War.

Prior to the arrival of Lupe Velez, Gonzalez had composed a waltz titled *Lupita* in her honor which was played at the Exchange Club's monthly luncheon and performed by the visiting Cuban band Sexteto Drana. The piece was met with thunderous applause.

As a playwright, he derived much of his subject matter from the world around him, using the day's current events as the main focus. He strived to create work that educationally entertained, and *La Pelicula de Rocky Point* was no exception. It was performed at the Temple of Labor Theater in Ybor City and contained songs written by Gonzalez with comedic monologues. It played to an audience of three hundred on October 20, 1929. Yet, it is doubtful that anyone from the actual Rocky Point movie attended the production.

16

A S if there were not enough movie stars milling about Tampa; on October 24th Gary Cooper came to town. He was there to visit Lupe Velez whom he was dating at the time. The relationship of the strong, silent Cooper and the vivacious Velez was fodder for the movie magazines. Their reunion caused the engines of the rumor and gossip mills — especially in Tampa— to go into overdrive as they speculated if the two would become engaged or even married while in town. The thought of a movie star descending from the sky to capture his lady's heart ignited the dreams of Tampa's romantics.

The in-demand actor, who made his film debut in *Wings* two years earlier had just finished one motion picture and found that, before the next one, he had a brief break, which he used to take a vacation. Cooper's itinerary was a full one. He first flew to his alma mater, Grinnell College in Iowa, where he was guest of honor at its homecoming celebrations. While there, he took part in the dedication of the new Grinnell airport. Later, he traveled to Chicago in order to visit some college friends living in the Windy City one of which was Harry Ogg, President of the Automatic Washer Company that later became Maytag. Ogg allowed his old friend to use "Smilin' Thru" his personal, specially equipped Travel Air monoplane so that Cooper could continue his sojourn to Florida. When he arrived at Lupe's door she cried out her pet name for him.

"Bepo! Is it really you?"

Despite the duration and hazards of the trip; Gary Cooper assured the journalists who were following him that he was simply making a social call to a very good friend. Lupe would reply in kind; shrugging her shoulders when asked if she was now engaged to Cooper.

The two "good friends" however, were obvious in their disguise. Reports of Lupe's vocal expressions of ecstasy that were heard throughout the 17th floor, when the two were alone, indicated a higher degree of personal pleasure far beyond "Good to see you." Days found Cooper on the set, fondly watching Velez work and socializing with cast members. In the evenings, the couple could be found riding through Tampa in the back of her cherry red, chauffeur driven limousine: sitting close, gazing at one another, and remaining oblivious to their surroundings.

Cooper left his timeframe in the area open and each day the same question was repeated numerous times: Are you engaged? He wanted to leave with Lupe, but her schedule would not permit it, forcing him to leave a few weeks before she was finished in order to get back to California. He would, however, stay for the shooting of the final scene.

One of the members of the cast that Gary Cooper befriended on the set of *Hell Harbor* was its youngest actor: George Bookasta. Their paths would cross again professionally twelve years later when the twenty-three-year old Bookasta was working as Gary Cooper's stand-in during the filming of *Sergeant York*. While that movie was in production, Bookasta's wife Laura gave birth to their first child; a son who would be named Gary, in honor of their friendship.

17

DURING the week of October 24th, the concluding fight scene of the picture would be captured on film. The action called for a number of special effects with violent choreography. For the type of camera work needed to film this battle royal, there was no one more experienced than John Fulton. He had been responsible for photographing the chilling battle scenes in *She Goes to War* for King, and the director had great faith in his abilities. The fight would take place in the El Marino and would include a mix of local extras, most of the male stars, and a few professional fighters culled from the gyms of Tampa.

Before there were major league sports teams in the city: Tampa's sport was boxing. Some of the best pugilists worldwide, with a formidable number from Cuba, would pass through the boxing rings of Tampa to spar with the local fighters. Joe Halloran, the young man that hitchhiked from California to work on the *Hell Harbor* set, sought to fight for a purse in the Welterweight Division prior to returning home.

On the night of September 20th, a local boxing promoter named George Kennedy reserved a private viewing area at Benjamin Field for boxing fanatic Lupe Velez and her friends. The venue was a large section of land previously donated by the city to the National Guard and where a wooden arena had been built for public boxing matches. Lupe arrived with

Henry King and his brother Louis. One of the fights on the card that night was a match between Herman Weiner and K.O. Billy Dugan. Wiener not only won the fight, but also a role in *Hell Harbor*.

Weiner grew up in East Baltimore, Maryland. He was twenty-three and a force with which to be reckoned. Eight months earlier he had knocked out the notorious Light Heavyweight World Champion, Battling Levinsky in under a minute during the first round. His dark hair and his height made him an excellent stand-in for John Holland.

While injuries were expected, the director did the best he could to keep them at a minimum and sought to keep everyone out of the hospital. After a number of rehearsals; starting in slow motion with direction as to how to throw and take punches, hurl objects, and generally break furniture, the time finally came to film the fight.

It was during one of those rehearsals that Holland was rushed to a local Osteopath after suffering a sprained neck and back. Because of his injuries, he required two stunt doubles: Weiner for the fight scenes and a local weather reporter named Bob Martin for the more acrobatic stunt of being thrown through a lattice window.

The special effects camera work of John Fulton is best demonstrated when, during the fight, Holland is punched and sent crashing through a lattice window. The angle is a close up of Holland's face and shoulders; quickly moving, arms flailing, almost levitating backward at high speed toward the window. It is the most creative shot in the film.

Another battle was also raging beyond Tampa that week:

one more violent than anything captured on film, and more devastating than the hurricane that nearly scuttled the production. Fought over 1500 miles away on the floor of the New York Stock Exchange, heavily margined buyers were in the death grip of short sellers. The forced sale of equity holdings led to a precipitous drop in stock prices and ultimately the evaporation of many investors personal wealth within a few hours. The poison cocktail of rumor, greed, and fear that was —and still remains— the lubricant of the stock speculation machine would end in the cessation of major investments for every U.S. industry including film financing, and give birth to The Great Depression which would afflict the economy of the United States for twelve years.

The final frame of *Hell Harbor* was to be of Bob Wade's schooner at full sail, gliding out to sea on the placid waters beneath it. This scene required a vast open ocean without any land on the horizon. It might, therefore, be necessary to photograph the ship in the Gulf of Mexico as opposed to Tampa Bay. One major problem existed: The Elsie was partly submerged in the waters off of Rocky Point; the damage to its hull made during the hurricane had finally taken its toll. It was now imperative to find another schooner that looked exactly like the Elsie.

18

S T. Petersburg, Florida lies west across the bay from the southern part of Tampa. The city had felt a great sense of disappointment in being left out of the production and desperately wanted some association with the movie. St. Petersburg was founded in1888 by John C. Williams a land speculator from Detroit, Michigan and Peter Demens, a railroad owner born in Russia. Demens named the settlement of roughly three hundred souls after the Russian city where he grew up.

St. Petersburg was much different than its neighbor across the bay. Its population was less than half of Tampa's, and because it did not have a port, there was a gentler feel about the place. The cities did, however, share in some important events together. On New Year's Day in 1914, the world's first commercial airline flight took place. A plane piloted by Tony Jannus flew former St. Petersburg mayor Abram Pheil over the bay to Tampa. Pheil had purchased the only ticket through an auction, paying $400.00 for the trip.

In 1924, the two cities would be physically joined together at one of the narrowest points in the bay by the Gandy Bridge. The publicity surrounding *Hell Harbor* and future of movies, however, was monopolized by Tampa. The sinking of the Elsie, St. Petersburg's city fathers believed, would open an opportunity for them and they were ready to act. A replacement schooner was found and the city immediately went into negotiations for filming. Both parties were eager to make a deal so signing the contract was just a formality, and within a few hours of the first meeting, there was an agreement.

The municipal pier at the end of downtown St. Petersburg was suggested as an ideal shooting location because it stood in, and was surrounded by, deep waters that could support any ship. There were also high tension power lines nearby to supply the electrical needs of the production. Known as the Million Dollar Pier, it had been opened to the public in 1926 after the original one had been destroyed in 1921 by a hurricane. The structure jutted 3000 feet into the bay and at its end had a multi-storied casino style building that could supply food and drinks to the crew. Its best advantage though, was that land could barely be seen in the distance making St. Petersburg the last stop for filming. The pier was co-managed by the St. Petersburg Library and the City Advertising Board, who in conjunction with the City Council and the Mayor's office, drew up a liberal agreement that allowed for three days of filming.

The promenade into the building would be roped off to foot traffic, but those wishing to watch the movie making would be allowed, at intervals, to enter the structure at the pier's end. Onlookers would not be allowed to speak between takes if they stood on the outside observation deck; so it was suggested they watch from inside the buildings thick glass.

The necessary cast and crew would arrive on the appointed days at 6:00 AM for filming at 8:00 AM. There would be few problems during these days, although at one point, Lupe Velez briefly experienced a bout of seasickness, finding comfort from Gary Cooper.

Since silence was required for these final scenes, Henry King ordered the raising of a red flag as a command to be quiet on the set. Even automobile engines on land, but within earshot of the filming, had to be turned off. King had become angry at one point that a number of small boats had delayed filming on Saturday with their motors and he asked the city to do something.

Finally, on a clear and sunny day with a deep blue sky and white clouds above them, Bob Wade's schooner drifted calmly on the glistening Florida waters. Having achieved the desired shot, Director Henry King yelled "Cut" and the camera stopped rolling. At that moment, on Sunday, November 3, the filming of *Hell Harbor* came to an end.

19

MOST of the players had left Tampa before the final scenes were shot. Lupe was asked to stay an extra week for some promotional photography and the making of a sound trailer. Along with her film work, she also found time to make civic appearances; her last being the annual Red Cross Roll Call membership drive.

On November 11th, her last day in Tampa, Velez visited the Rocky Point set one last time. It was during a stroll among the buildings and looking out at the sunrise over the waters, that she met Margaret Benke walking her white bulldog. The spontaneous star fell in love with the pet and offered to purchase it on the spot. After a number of refusals by Mrs. Benke, a price of $150.00 was finally agreed upon.

That same night Lupe Velez: movie star, Queen of the Ball, and an idol to a countless number of Tampa's women and men, left the city with her personal assistant Helene Ruppert; two trunk loads of clothes purchased in the city, and a new dog that she named Coconito.

Not far from the train station was the Burgert Brothers Photography Studio; the home of Tampa's preeminent photographers. Their cameras had photographically chronicled the growth of the city, the faces of its residents, and most of its newsworthy events since 1897. Located on Madison Street in the heart of downtown, the studio contained the most advanced darkroom and photofinishing equipment in the area. Because of this reputation, Henry King, and his Film Editor, Lloyd Nosler chose to rent and occupy The Burgert Brother's studio for almost a month in order to make the final edits to the movie: chiseling from a mountain of film, the final set of images that the world would see as *Hell Harbor*.

Nosler was a film editing legend. His resume included the silent epic *Ben-Hur* (1925), The John Gilbert, Greta Garbo vehicle *Flesh and the Devil* (1926), and Henry King's, *She Goes to War* (1929). He would continue to edit films throughout the 1930s. In the early 1960s he began a career in television, working on programs like *77 Sunset Strip*, *Maverick*, and *Hawaiian Eye*.

During the filming of *Hell Harbor*, many local newspaper reporters gave day by day coverage of the scenes being shot and their outcomes. However, much of their reportage was changed in the editing room. Six lost minutes could explain some of the deletions. The original theatrical running time was ninety minutes, but the only known 35 mm print in existence runs eighty-four minutes. All that is left of the in full theatrical release is the soundtrack and that does not show the visuals.

The street scene with Ruth Ybañez, appears to be lost, as does the acrobatic work of Al St. John swinging from a chandelier in the final fight. Some scenes were shot with different conclusions from which only one could be selected. A scene vividly described in the October 24th issue of the *Tampa Morning Tribune* tells of the murder of Blinky at the hand of Gibson Gowland. In the theatrical release, Blinky survives the violent fight.

When King was not shut away from the world in the editing room, he was speaking to it. Always a believer in his product, the director either talked about the superiority of his motion picture or the beauty of Tampa; always underscoring its soon-to-be-place as a modern movie capital. In an interview with the *Tampa Morning Tribune* on November 4, 1929, the director is quoted:

"I believe it will be one of the greatest all talking pictures ever produced...But I have several reasons for my prediction. First... the beauty of the natural surroundings. When this picture is released, I believe the critics will praise its beauty in their comments as much or more than any other characteristic."

King felt an obligation to Tampa for the outpouring of goodwill he received during the production and wanted to repay it. He would leave the city with the final cut on December 5, 1929, and return to Hollywood so that Tec-Art Studios could create the titles and opening credits. He promised to return to Tampa after the New Year and express his gratitude by hosting the world premiere of *Hell Harbor* at one of its theaters. This act of recognition would elevate Tampa from a backdrop of beautiful scenery to a city on par with New York or Los Angeles for the showcasing of movies.

In the mind of Henry King, *Hell Harbor* was more than a movie, it was an innovation. There were 8,000 feet of film in the final cut, and if it proved to be a successful all-talking feature, made far from California, then it would show that the use of expensive studios or sound stages could be eliminated. Productions could be self-contained, movies less expensive to make, and cities across the country would reap a number of financial and public relations benefits.

20

WHILE the electric company was removing the wires it extended to Rocky Point, and the once hectic motion picture set stood in quiet rest. Among the serene silence with only to the gentle serenade of the lapping waves that rhythmically broke on the shore before it; Joe Polaco examined his fiefdom.

Polacco was a tenant on the island. He lived in the only house on Rocky Point, which was located on its southernmost tip. An entrepreneur, he owned the only soft drink concession stand on the beach during filming. Others had specialty booths there as well; like Esteban Pellon, who rented boats, and whose daughter, Margaret doubled for Lupe Velez in a scene where Anita dives from the schooner. Polacco was the caretaker of the island and it was he that set out to restore the area after everyone left; burning trash and removing the detritus of the production.

The Elsie lay partly on the beach, exposing the large gaping hole underneath that rendered it useless. The vessel that once proudly sailed the waters of Tampa Bay, the Gulf of Mexico and the Caribbean was sold by the movie company for $50.00 to Steven Kissenger, the harbor patrolman who had helped preserve the set during the hurricane.

One week after Lupe Velez left for California, another tenant would temporarily move onto the island. Relampago Saguero was the Cuban Junior Welterweight Champion, known as "The Lighting from Camaguey". He was scheduled to fight ten rounds with Tampa born boxer Young Manuel Quintero "The Spanish Hurricane" on November 30, 1929. This was to be the second bout between the two pugilists. The first ended in a questionable defeat of Saguero before six thousand fans, the largest attendance ever at Benjamin Field. The two men felt honor bound to settle the doubts and agreed to another match.

In Ybor City, where Saguero worked out, there were constant distractions: noise, food, and the useless public advice on how to jab were wearing thin on him. The fighter decided to take his training facility to Rocky Point and move into the hut Lupe Velez used as her dressing room. He built his own boxing ring by the water, ran along its shores, and incorporated the climbing of palm trees into his regimen. There was a marked change in Saguero, and he owed it all to the solitude of Hell Harbor.

The rest of Tampa had grown quiet too, in much the same way a house gets quiet after company leaves. The citizenry went about their daily routines: the banker banked, the cigar roller rolled, the cook cooked, and the tailor tailored. No longer were there celebrity sightings of Lupe Velez enjoying paella at her favorite Spanish restaurant after a shopping spree, or of Al St. John slipping into a movie theater to catch a show. Conversations turned to more pressing matters; among them, the winning Bollita numbers, President Herbert Hoover, and of course, the upcoming Saguero-Quintero fight: A battle that would be won at the end of November by Quintero.

Then, on the evening of January 7, 1930, Trent Collins received a wire from United Artists press agent Lou Lusty. The meaning of the message was clear: Get ready, *Hell Harbor* is coming. This was the realization of something very big. No film had ever had its premiere anywhere in the southern United States and with this decision; Tampa would be once again considered a city of cinematic firsts. There was, however, a bit of consternation regarding the venue. United Artists had scheduled the premiere at the Victory Theater in downtown Tampa. The city would have preferred that the event take place at the Tampa Theater. The Victory was popular, but it was nearly a decade older; while the Tampa Theater, built in 1926, was the crown jewel of the city's movie houses.

A creation of famed theater architect John Eberson, the interior gave audiences a sense that they were sitting outside, under the clear evening sky of an Italian Renaissance palazzo, or a Moorish influenced Spanish courtyard; complete with a twinkling starlight ceiling, faux balconied windows, and plenty of statues standing in grottos along the wall and around the screen. The theater had also been the first choice for the premiere and early ticket sales were based on its seating chart. A few weeks later, in a surprise move, United Artists made the decision to move the event to the Victory despite the protests from Tampa.

The wire from Lusty instructed Collins to connect with Guy Kenimer, general manager of the Publix Organization that owned the Victory and to visit Thomas Meighan at his home in New Port Richey. Collins was to deliver a personal invitation to the man that recommended the area to Henry King. In a few weeks, the actor would also be visited by Gloria Swanson and the invitation should be extended to her as well. A third person would also travel to New Port Richey with Kenimer and Collins; he was Jerome Waterman, President of Maas Brothers Department Stores, and an early booster of films to the area.

The Chamber of Commerce was in charge of hosting the event and doing the preparations in conjunction with Lou Lusty, who had returned to Tampa on January 16th and had set up an office in the Floridan Hotel. The Chamber sought higher ticket prices for the premiere, but Henry King rejected any amount over $2.00. It was finally agreed upon that seats on the main floor and the first tier of the balcony would be sold for $2.00. Patrons paying this admission price would also receive a commemorative hardbound book featuring photographs of the production, a complete retelling of the film's storyline, and plaudits to the people of Tampa for their hospitality. The remaining two hundred, second tier balcony seats would be sold for $1.50 without any additional perks. United Artists and Inspiration Pictures arranged to have cameras on hand to record the red carpet event, and local radio station WDAE would broadcast it live to its listeners, interviewing notables and celebrities as they entered the lobby.

The first print of the movie arrived in Tampa on January 22nd and was heavily guarded by the theater. As a precautionary measure, Henry King would also carry a second print with him when he arrived by train on the morning of the premiere: January 24th. Prior to his arrival, King had asked that all banquets, lunches, and personal appearances scheduled for him on the day of the premiere be canceled. He wanted to spend the entire day at the theater, making sure that everything was perfect before the premiere. After hours in the darkness of the Victory, he emerged satisfied that his film and its venue were ready. Now, as the Florida sun was declining, he would briefly rest, then put on his tuxedo, and begin the worry and anticipation of the project's debut.

****

The premiere was scheduled for 8:30. Henry King arrived early with his wife, the former silent star Gypsy Abbott. Mayor McKay and Thomas Meighan were there as was comic actor Leon Errol who would later portray Uncle Matt Lindsey opposite Lupe Velez in all of her franchise *Mexican Spitfire* films in the 1940s. Remarkably, not one of the *Hell Harbor* stars that so recently set the city aglow could make the premiere. This, however, did not faze the people of Tampa. They understood that the glamorous Hollywood crowd had moved on with their own lives just as they had. Tonight was not about them anyway: It was about the local people who had parts in the film, it was about the beauty of their environs, and it was about their hometown's place in the future of dreams. Movie stars at this moment would just be in the way of Tampa's own luster.

Before the lights dimmed, Carl Brorein of the chamber stood center stage and welcomed everyone. He then introduced Mayor McKay who told Henry King that he hoped that the movie would be a success and that he would return to make more movies. Thomas Meighan was then asked to speak; being introduced as the man that suggested King visit Florida. Meighan extolled the area, telling the crowd that there was no reason that Tampa should not have a place in the pantheon of movie capitals.

"California has no more than Florida," he said. "The first picture I made in California was in a livery stable. You have here all you need. And all you need now is a few live wire citizens to get out and hustle."

Henry King spoke next. He thanked the people of Tampa for their hospitality and in particular, Mayor McKay's participation. Before he could leave the stage, chamber member Burks Hamner walked on bearing a number of telegrams sent to the Chamber of Commerce which he shared with King and the audience. Governor Carlton apologized for not being there. Every member of the cast individually expressed their sadness for not being present but sent their best wishes. Others sending congratulations were: Producers Joseph Schenck and Adolf Zukor; King's partner at Inspiration Pictures, Richard Barthelmas; United Artists was represented by Lillian Gish, Charlie Chaplin, Mary Pickford, and Douglas Fairbanks; the great acrobatic comedian Harold Lloyd sent his best wishes as did the composer, Irving Berlin and actor Ronald Coleman. Even Dolores Del Rio, with whom Lupe had an ongoing feud, and Lupe's best friend, Fannie Brice sent salutations.

After the reading of the telegraphs, Carl Brorein

presented Henry King with a gold watch on behalf of the City and People of Tampa. The director was surprised and was visibly moved by this unexpected gesture. He held it up and told everyone that the watch was doubly meaningful to him because this day was also his birthday.

As the lights went down and the flickering images of the title appeared on the theater screen the audience began to clap but then catching itself, quickly stopped and remained quiet: because *Hell Harbor* was a movie to be seen and heard. The first opening shots of the palm trees at Rocky Point silently excited the crowd. They were drawn in by the sound of Harry Allen's wooden leg as it beat in cadence with his stride, to be met shortly by the squeaking of Hersholt's shoes when he reached his destination. They listened with rapt attention to the commerce between Peg Leg and the merchant, and they followed the action to the El Marino Cafe where the mood of the audience became more animated. Seeing their friends and neighbors dancing and cavorting to the sound of a son band reminded many of the Cuba they left and others of the Cuba they imagined. There was laughter and applause, names were called out and fingers pointed at the onscreen performers in the dark. They watched locals pour and serve drinks, gamble at cards or just stand idly inebriated. Proper young ladies that went to dances at the Centro Espanol, Centro Asturiano, or the Circulo Cubano with their dueñas, were seen flirting and hustling with sailors and fighters. They watched Rondo Hatton stare menacingly at his patrons, and everyone loved every minute of the make-believe decadence. There was a sense of pride among the audience members for knowing, or being related to one of the extras. The party atmosphere so vividly created onscreen spilled into the theater but came to a somber end with the murder of Peg Leg by Henry Morgan.

And so it went for the duration of the movie: the highs, lows, fears, and frolics that were performed on the screen were transmitted and absorbed into the psyches of the viewers. When the last frame of film containing Bob Wade's schooner on the tranquil waters off of St. Petersburg had finally dissolved, and all that was left on the screen were the words: THE END, a thunderous ovation shook the walls of the Victory Theater. Henry King, triumphant and hungry, left the theater for a victory dinner at the El Pasaje Restaurant in Ybor City with his wife, the Meighans, the Collins, Lou Lusty, Guy Kenimer and some other friends.

The film was a success in the eyes of the audience that night as well. New York would have to wait until March for their premiere, followed by the rest of the country, and then the world. Floridians believed that their state would be recognized for more than orange trees and alligators. The moving pictures of the new era would combine the attributes of sight, sound, and sunshine to make Florida — and more specifically Tampa— synonymous with movie making. It was now just a matter of time before other producers would look to the area.

In Sebring, Florida; a small rural town approximately 100 miles from Tampa, the premiere of a second film took place a few weeks later. *Son of the Gods* starring Richard Barthelmes and Constance Bennett had its debut showing at the Circle Theater on February 9, 1930. While the movie was neither photographed in Sebring nor was the city alluded to in any way in the film, its claim to recognition was that Rex Beach, the author of the book on which the movie was adapted, was a resident of the quiet Florida town. Other than Beach's personal introduction of the film that night, there was no advanced promotion or fanfare by Warner Brothers' distribution team for the event. In its own small way, though, the second premiere of a movie in Florida only underscored the beginning rivalry of the Sunshine State with the Golden State of California.

21

NEEDLESS to say, the critics in Tampa lavished high praise on the movie made in their hometown. They cheered like a parent cheers on a child at a recital. Their reviews found no faults within the film and boasted only of its merits. Having followed its progress almost daily from idea to finished product, and seeing one of their own fellow newspapermen made a member of the cast, it could be easily assumed that there was a bias built into the Tampa reviews. This may have been true to a degree, but the comments about the film were fair and reasonable. The lionizing of the leading lady's loveliness, the accolades on Hersholt's acting prowess and the praise for exceptional sound and scenery would have been within reason had they been written by someone not as closely associated with the production. The movie magazine *Cinema* actually singled out the *Tampa Daily Times* and the *Tampa Tribune* for its excellent reporting on the production.

Other national periodicals dispensed accolades: *Screenland* magazine awarded *Hell Harbor* its coveted Blue Ribbon designation, calling it one of the six best movies of the month and something different from the usual Hollywood fare. *Photoplay* concurred in their selection, also citing the beautiful scenery and photography. More people in Tampa had seen *Hell Harbor* in one week than any other movie that ever played in the city. The real test, however, would be how the New York critics opined on the pages of their newspapers;

leaving Henry King and United Artists counting the days until the film's premiere at Broadway's Rialto Theater on March 27, 1930.

The anticipated reviews that followed were mostly disappointing. Quinn Martin of the *New York World* hailed director King's ability to "capture the photographic beauty" around him but called the story "halting, tedious, humorless without the merit tendency to be dramatic."

The *New York Herald's* Richard Watt wrote that *Hell Harbor* had "The worst narrative and the best atmospheric photography of the season."

Mordaunt Hall, the movie critic for *The New York Times* praised the scenery but felt that the director had spent too much time on clouds and not enough on the plot. He also specifically, if not unfairly, derided King's tracking shot of the band's instruments at the El Marino as too long. Hall's failure to see beyond the film's story and see the film's purpose is difficult to understand. Since *Hell Harbor* was the first film to combine the sense of sound with the visuals of an exotic location; it was just as important to show how and from where the melodies of this idyllic place emanated —especially when the music was coming from so many strange and foreign instruments that much of the movie-going public had never seen.

There were a few reviews that favored the film. Martin Dickstein's column, *The Cinema Circuit* in *The Brooklyn Daily Eagle* called *Hell Harbor,* "A picture of countless visual delights." Despite his reservations about the faults he saw in the script, Dickstein closed his review by saying that "fine acting and captivating photography help to overcome them."

Regina Crewe of the *New York American* was unequivocal in her praise stating that "*Hell Harbor* is... a forthright bit of entertainment" and that Henry King should be credited for producing such "a fine piece of work."

One of the best reviews came from *Los Angeles Times* critic Edwin Schallert who penned that: "*Hell Harbor* gains by its colorful characters and their equally colorful impersonators." He further commented, "This production is a good old-time melodrama, with the benefit of a rare exotic setting, tropical atmosphere, and good sound effects and dialogue... It is one of the best "melos" that has yet to come to the sound shadow stage."

The critics had spoken, and for the most part, the one thing that they could agree upon was the beauty of the location. *Hell Harbor,* despite its faults, had showcased Tampa in a light as favorable as the Florida summer sun. The vessel may have had a few cracks, but the wine inside was still good.

Once that the movie was finished it was now up to Tampa to continue the momentum on its own. The time of directors and actors, movie sets and movie crews was over —at least for now. The Chamber of Commerce reported that they had been contacted by other production companies and were still under the belief that Henry King would make *Beautiful Music* at Rocky Point. The mood of Tampa was optimistic and the future seemed unstoppable.

22

THE future did not play out well for Tampa after the premiere. The national box office receipts for *Hell Harbor* were lackluster and, because of this, studios were reticent to go on location due to costs. There was still a better margin of profitability producing a picture on a soundstage or on a location in California than moving across the country. Henry King had proven that an all talking motion picture could be made with exterior shots somewhere other than Burbank, but the technology was still rudimentary and expensive. Studio heads saw the future, but it was not now. The Great Depression was also a factor. Many investors lost their fortunes in the stock market collapse a year earlier and funds were tight in Hollywood.

Tampa would discover that the dreamers of Hollywood often spoke through the haze of their own burning egos and imagination. They brought interesting ideas that seemed to evaporate in the light of reality and projects that would never materialize. When it was obvious that *Beautiful Music* would not be made on Rocky Point, or anywhere else, and that interest from other studios had waned, a monocle-wearing specter from the past came back to Tampa.

Count Phillip d'Esco, the prop man, announced that he had come to inspect the set. He told the press that he was there because negotiations were underway to film a Spanish language version of *Hell Harbor*. The new movie would only have one of the original stars; d'Esco did not say who the star was, but it did not take much to conclude who it might be. The rest of the cast, he stated, would be made up of people from Ybor City and West Tampa. Because the Latin American and Spanish markets were enormous, and their hunger for new films was no secret, the Count's story was more than credible. After the inspection, he would go to New York where the investors were trying to secure the rights to remake *Hell Harbor*. Apparently though, a deal could not be struck because the movie was never made.

The Chamber of Commerce began an uphill walk. Money for publicity dried up from the City of Tampa and Hillsborough County. The Chamber was forced to pay all of the out of pocket printing costs for brochures touting the area. The advice of Thomas Meighan seemed to be ignored: All that was needed were a few live wires to continue bringing movies to Tampa. The wires were plugged in but sadly, there was no more electricity.

For a brief time, Rocky Point was referred to as Hell Harbor and the set became a tourist attraction. Those wishing to get an up-close view and a tour of the buildings could do so for a small emolument to one of the island merchants. Along the way the sandy, sun-splashed docents would share firsthand accounts of the movie stars that once wandered the beach while making the movie. A number of social clubs and business organizations held their annual fetes at the abandoned set, the most robust of which was Centro Asturiano's July 1930 fundraiser that lasted twenty-four hours and accommodated ten thousand guests.

In 1932 Trenton Collins was the appointed Chairman of the Committee for the Development of the Motion Picture Industry (CDMP). A state organization firmly endorsed by Governor Doyle Carlton. The purpose of the organization was to attract producers and directors to use Florida as a location for their films. It was during this time, that Chester Beecroft came to Tampa.

Beecroft was a character. He had been an actor on Broadway and during his life, he worked as a newspaperman, public relations manager, theatrical agent, and even took part in an arctic expedition. He saw the future of movies while working as the General Manager of Cosmopolitan Studios owned by newspaperman William Randolph Hearst. It was his tenure at Cosmopolitan that inspired him to become a mogul within the industry.

Beecroft decided to build his own studio in Florida because of its California-like climate and its proximity to New York (a mere 11 hours by plane at the time). He undoubtedly chose Tampa for the obvious reasons that were bolstered by the salesmanship of his guide, Trenton Collins: Namely, the area's weather, resources, and prior film experience. Beecroft was taken to the Davis Island Coliseum, which was one of the largest buildings in the southern United States, and the budding movie entrepreneur envisioned dividing it into four soundstages complete with dressing rooms, and editing facilities. Cash-strapped Tampa offered him a long-term lease and an option to buy the building. The estimate to convert the structure would be $100,000. No time was wasted in getting started once pen was put to paper, and shortly after

the signing, construction crews went to work making alterations while film equipment was being delivered.

Tampa watched in excitement as Chester Beecroft threw
himself into the community; hosting beauty contests and
throwing lavish Balls where guests could take screen and
voice tests to be considered for future movie roles. The
Mayor of Tampa, Robert E. Lee Chancey, saw the arrival
of the studio as a lifeline and enthusiastically welcomed it.
The city's revenue had been drastically reduced due to the
Depression, and painful cuts were being made to services.
Finally, the dream of turning Tampa into a money-making
movie capital seemed to be imminent.

Rondo Hatton was hired to handle publicity for the
Beecroft-Florida Corporation. Two weeks after leasing the
Coliseum, Beecroft took control of the Davis Island Golf
Course and began making improvements on its greens. All of
this growth was based on the success of an idea and a month
later the idea was revealed.

Chester Beecroft wanted to make a film version of the
Broadway comedy *Diamond Lil,* casting its star and writer,
Mae West in the lead. The picture would be the first film for
both West and the fledgling studio. Beecroft recognized the
talent of West as well as the power of her persona. He fully
understood that her participation would grant legitimacy to
his venture and allow him to attract larger talent. She understood that film was the next step in her career despite the fact
that Will Hayes, head of the Motion Pictures Producers and
Distributors of America, was encouraging major studios not
to sign her because of her risqué act.

Beecroft approached the actress with a three-year contract and she signed. The financing was almost complete but was still short $15,000.00. The acquisition of Mae West as a formal studio talent was believed by Beecroft to be the magnet that would draw the remaining amount from investors. The actress began making arrangements to bring her props to Tampa, including a $40,000 bed given to her by "Diamond" Jim Brady.

Unfortunately, the additional money could not be raised and the deal that looked so secure slipped through the hands of Chester Beecroft. Mae West was released from her obligation and was signed by Paramount. *Diamond Lil* was brought to the screen as *She Done Him Wrong* and made two million dollars for the studio. Other Mae West films followed under the Paramount banner and each was a financial success. Beecroft-Florida eventually shuttered its doors.

In his last Tampa interview before he returned to California, Chester Beecroft said dejectedly:

"Every time I saw a billing of *She Done Him Wrong* I felt sick all over. That was an opportunity of a lifetime and all that stood between us was the $15,000.00 we could not raise."

Except for a few second unit scenes filmed around MacDill Air Force Base in the 1940's and Paramount's shots of Al Lang Field in 1955's *Strategic Air Command,* the city of Tampa would wait thirty-five years after the 1929 filming of *Hell Harbor* before it would once again be prominently featured in another major motion picture. That film was 1964's, *Black Like Me* which was photographed partly in Ybor

City and the surrounding areas. Burt Reynold's comedy, *Cop & ½* made in 1993 could qualify as the first major movie in 64 years to be entirely shot in Tampa.

23

BY the end of Tampa's active tropical storm season of 1930, the set at Rocky Point lay in ruins. Its destruction was the final curtain of a show that brought so much excitement and pleasure to the city. The world was changing and lives, thoughts, and philosophies moved forward with it.

In 1934 Rocky Point would be bisected by the Davis Causeway which linked Clearwater, a city situated ten miles to the west across the bay to Tampa in the east. The causeway would eventually become a part of Florida State Highway 60 that would connect Clearwater Beach on the Gulf of Mexico to Vero Beach on the Atlantic Ocean. The Davis Causeway was built by Ben T. Davis as a .25¢ toll road. It was eventually purchased by the federal government in 1944 and then ownership was transferred to the State of Florida. Four years later it was renamed the Courtney Campbell Causeway after a U.S. Representative and member of the Florida State Road Department that led a causeway beautification project and oversaw needed repairs. As can be expected, the name change did not sit well with the Davis family.

By 1940, a decade years after its premiere, *Hell Harbor,* the movie, lay in a can, on a shelf, in a studio archive unseen for many years; consigned to the crypt of forgotten films. *Hell Harbor,* the phenomenon, still retained its place as a part of Tampa's folklore, but even to those who experienced its grandeur, found their fond memories gradually being relegated behind the more pressing matters that develop with life; their once vivid images soon began fading like a painting in the hot Florida sun.

Movies had changed as well: sound was a given and no longer a novelty. Technicolor improved on the visuals, and Hollywood was seen as the only undisputed capital of filmdom glamour.

The Floridan Hotel that once was the temporary palace of movie stars began to experience a decline in the 1960s. As populations shifted from downtown urban areas to suburbs, the hotel guests stopped coming. The once magnificent jewel of the skyline was turned into a residential hotel in the 1970s that rented its rooms at $30.00 per week to people that could generally not afford them. The Floridan eventually closed and sat vacant until 2012 when a new owner refurbished it and restored it to its past glory.

The Tampa Theater, where *She Goes to War* was last seen in its original form and where Lupe Velez performed, was slated for demolition in 1973. The people of Tampa rallied to save the landmark and it stands today as a glittering link to the past.

Ybor City saw its cigar factories close or automate, eliminating the need for hand rollers. The second and third generations of immigrant families that once lived there were assimilated into the mainstream and moved away. The historic section of town that once hosted the Cuban Liberator Jose Marti fell into decline.

In the 1920s and '30s, Ybor City had been the home to countless restaurants, but by 2019 only one from the era remains. *The Columbia* has stood at its 7th Avenue location since 1905 and its longevity is a testament to its time-tested traditional Spanish menu and the leadership of its innovative and theatrical owner Cesar Gonzmart.

A Tampa-born, classically trained violinist, Gonzmart was brought into the restaurant business in 1953 when he married a fellow musician and Juilliard graduate Adela Hernandez; who was the granddaughter of the Columbia's founder and daughter of its then-current owner.

Under Gonzmart's tutelage, the restaurant expanded but a great challenge came during the late 1960s and 1970s when Ybor City fell into the spiral of urban decline. The families that were the bedrock of the ethnic enclave began to move out, and the once vibrant area became an abyss with a fading past and little hope of a future. It was at this time that the Columbia Restaurant positioned itself as a shining bastion of Spanish and Cuban culture, providing expertly prepared meals and entertainment by some of Spain's best showmen and musical troupes. There were very few reasons to visit Ybor City in the evening at that time, but having dinner at The Columbia was the exception.

On nights when musical entertainment was not being imported, Gonzmart personally entertained his guests by playing the violin along with an accompanying house band. It is notable that his showmanship also earned him a small place in Tampa movie history as well. In 1987, a made for television baseball movie was filmed in Tampa called *Long Gone*. In one of its final scenes, Cesar Gonzmart, along with members of his band, can be seen performing *The Wedding March* for Virginia Madsen and William Petersen.

In the 1990s a revitalization campaign began to breathe new life into the area and Tampa continued to expand without the movie industry. Mayor D.B. McKay no longer ran for a mayoral office, but in 1949 he was appointed Hillsborough County's Historian and wrote a newspaper column called *Pioneer Florida* until his death in 1960.

Carl Brorein merged his Peninsular Telephone Company with General Systems to create the General Telephone Company of Florida in 1957. He remained active in Tampa organizations. He died at age 87 in 1973.

Trenton Collins continued to work in public relations as a sales promotion manager for Maas Brothers and later operated his own advertising agency. He died in Colorado in 1968.

Rocky Point is unrecognizable from its *Hell Harbor* days. There is now a seawall where the beach once slopped into the water and office buildings, hotels and residences cover what was once a serene island.

Rocky Point has once more been brought into the future.

24

HENRY KING
(Director)

HENRY King remained one of the most distinguished and respected directors in Hollywood throughout a career that spanned six decades.

"I've had more fun directing pictures than most people have playing games." He once commented.

King enjoyed the movie business, and he was good at it. He directed over 115 films and was known to innovate and recognize talent early on. When he made *The White Sister,* in 1923, the director painted a mustache on the male lead, Ronald Coleman. Coleman was so impressed with his look that he grew and maintained the same pencil-thin facial hair, making it his trademark.

With the same innate sense that he used to recognize Jean Hersholt's ability to play Horngold in *Hell Harbor* when no one else could see it, King fostered other actors and was responsible for advancing Tyrone Power and Gregory Peck early in their careers. He cast Power in eleven pictures including; *Lloyd's of London* (1936), *In Old Chicago* (1938), *Alexander's Ragtime Band* (1938), *Jesse James* (1939), *Captain from Castile* (1947), and an adaptation of Ernest Hemingway's novel *The Sun Also Rises* (1957). Gregory Peck appeared in seven features; *Twelve O'clock High* (1947), *The Gunfighter* (1950), Hemingway's *The Snows of Kilimanjaro* (1953), and *Beloved Infidel* (1959).

He also worked well with many of Hollywood's established actors like Spencer Tracy in *Stanley and Livingston* (1939), William Holden and Jennifer Jones in *Love Is A Many Splendored Thing* (1953) and Jason Robards in, *Tender is the Night* (1962) which was King's last film. In 1957, he directed the screen version of the Broadway musical, *Carousel,* once again making use of the glory of sound.

A Founding Member of the Academy of Motion Picture Arts and Sciences, King never received an Oscar for his work, although he did receive two nominations; one for *Song of Bernadette* in 1944 and for *Wilson* in 1945.

Along with a successful career, King also had a successful marriage for 38 years to silent film actress Gypsy Abbott which produced three children. A native of Atlanta, Georgia, Abbot made seven films with King while he was working as an actor. They were wed in 1914 and she appeared in one King's early directorial efforts; an episode the serial *Who Pays?* in 1915. She retired from acting in 1917, supporting her husband throughout his career. She attended the premiere of *Hell Harbor* with him in Tampa. In 1952, a heart attack ended her life and was interred at Holy Cross Cemetery in Culver City, California.

King was known as "The Flying Director" because of his skill in the cockpit of a plane and when he died at age 96, he was the oldest person to hold a pilot's license. After his retirement from moviemaking, King traveled the country by plane and often returned to Tampa and Clearwater to fish and play golf. He maintained friendships with Trenton Collins and fellow flying enthusiast Jerome Watterman, the Chairman of Maas Brothers Department Stores. Watterman was a pioneer in aviation and his license to fly was actually signed by Orville Wright.

During one of his trips to Tampa, King was introduced to Ida Davis. Davis was born in Smyrna, Tennessee and was a relative of Confederate hero Sam Davis known as "The Boy Hero of the Confederacy". She was raised in Tampa where her family ran a business and where she lived the life of a debutant. In 1932, she married a commercial artist named Robert Batey, and the couple moved to New York City. When that marriage ended, Ida returned to Tampa and worked as a fashion buyer for Maas Brothers. She was also heavily involved with philanthropic work in the area. Henry King and Ida Davis were married in Riverside, California in 1959. Their marriage would last twenty-three years.

Henry King died in his sleep on June 29, 1982, at his home in Toluca Lake, California in a house that had once been the residence of Amelia Earhart. The home was purchased by Ida as a surprise for her aviator husband.

Ida returned to Tampa, passing away on March 24, 2001. She is interred with Henry King in the Davis-King family mausoleum at Myrtle Hill Cemetery in Tampa.

25

HARRY ALLEN
(Peg Leg)

HARRY Radford Allen died at his home in Van Nuys, California in 1951 leaving behind a wife and two grown children. He had appeared in small movie roles and performed on the stage in London and New York. While not a well-known name in motion pictures, he was ubiquitous. Allen can be found as a crew member in 1935's *Mutiny on the Bounty* and as a doorman in the Marx Brothers; *A Night at the Opera*. He was the taxi driver in *Waterloo Bridge* (1940), and a baseball player in *Take Me Out to the Ball Game* (1949). He made two more additional films with Henry King; *Lloyds of London* (1936) where he played a waiter and *A Yank in the R.A.F.* (1941) where he appears as an Air Raid Warden. He acted in nearly 118 films during a career that spanned nearly thirty years after leaving Australia.

26

JEAN HERSHOLT
(Joseph Horngold)

WITHOUT argument, the actor with the longest and most distinguished career after *Hell Harbor* was Jean Hersholt. The accent that almost destroyed his career became an asset; casting him in the roles of Austrian professors, French doctors, and Germans of all stripes.

After *Hell Harbor*, Henry King and Jean Hersholt were under contract with different studios and did not work together again until 1936 when King was able to cast his friend in another career shaping movie, *The Country Doctor*. The film tells the story of the Dionne Quintuplets of Canada and their physician Dr. John Luke. The Danish actor portrayed the trials and tribulations of the struggling doctor practicing medicine in a poor French Canadian lumber town. The film also featured the quintuplets who had less screen time but received top billing. Hersholt enjoyed the part and reprised his role in two sequels that were not directed by King: *Reunion* (1936) and *Five of A Kind* (1938).

As he worked on the various projects, Hersholt began to formulate in his mind, an entire series centered on Doctor Luke that focused on his ability to dispense medical care and folksy wisdom to a small rural community. The legal rights to proceed with such a project, however, could not be secured by the actor. Undaunted, Hersholt created his own character, Dr. Christian, a country doctor that lived in a small midwestern town in the United States.

The rural adventures of the kindly doctor were first performed as a radio program in 1937 and continued until 1954. There were six Dr. Christian films made between 1939 and 1941 and a novel, *Dr. Christian's Office* that was co-authored by Hersholt and Ruth Adams Knight in 1943. It is interesting to note that the small part Mrs. Sam in *The Courageous Dr. Christian*, made in 1940, is played by Sylvia Andrew, the first wife of Gibson Gowland.

A steady workload over the years and wise investing made Hersholt a very wealthy man. He dedicated a large percentage of his earnings and time to charitable causes and personally volunteered his time. His greatest accomplishment came while he was serving as President of The Motion Picture Relief Fund; an organization developed to help those in the movie industry that had become destitute. It was under his leadership that the Motion Picture Country House and Hospital was built (later to be known as The Motion Picture and Television Country House and Hospital).

In 1957, because of Hersholt's efforts, the Academy of Motion Picture Arts and Sciences began bestowing the Jean Hersholt Humanitarian Award at Oscar time to someone who has exemplified a spirit of service in support of humanitarian causes.

Along with his reputation as an actor and philanthropist,

Hersholt was also a renowned scholar on the subject of Danish writer Hans Christian Andersen. He translated into English all of Andersen's stories; compiling them into six volumes considered to be the definitive collection. Partly for this effort, in 1948, King Frederick IX of Denmark presented Hersholt with a Knighthood in the Order of Danneborg. The honor is granted for contributions to the world by Danes.

In 1956, Hersholt died of cancer shortly after his last appearance on the television series *Dr. Christian*. The beloved character had been interpreted by its creator in print, radio, film, and finally the new medium of television. The veteran actor of nearly 150 films had a career that spanned half a century; starting in the nascent days of the movie industry, and ending with the dawn of television. He is buried in Forest Lawn Memorial Park in Glendale, California. His grave is marked by a sculpture of *Clumsy Hans*, a character from a Hans Christian Andersen fairy tale who won the hand of a princess over many more accomplished suitors in spite of himself, simply by being himself.

27

RONDO HATTON
(Bouncer at the El Marino Cafe)

WITH the collapse of Beecroft Studios, Rondo Hatton found himself at a crossroad. He had wanted to be involved in the motion picture industry, but it had become painfully obvious that Tampa was not going to be the place to pursue those ambitions.

During the filming of *Hell Harbor,* Henry King had been impressed with and spoke highly of the amateur actor's ability to immerse himself in a scene. The seasoned director also advised Hatton that his unique physical appearance would be more of an asset than a liability when approaching casting directors and offered to assist the news reporter in any way should he ever decide to come to Hollywood.

Hatton eventually made up his mind: He would go to California and contact King. Before he left, however, there was someone with whom he wanted to share the journey. Someone who had encouraged and strengthened him in many of his soul's darkest moments. Someone whose light and inspiration he needed: Her name was Mabel Housh.

Mabel Housh was an attractive divorcee of twenty-seven who was working as a seamstress and dressmaker in Tampa. She met Hatton while he was covering a costume party for the *Tampa Tribune*, and where she had done some last minute alterations on the dress of the hostess. The two began a conversation and were inseparable from that moment. From Mabel, Hatton learned that being plagued with Acromegly was different than being consumed by it. Life had to be lived, and though Hatton understood that the disease was ultimately a death sentence, it did not have to carry with it a life in solitary confinement. On September 29, 1934, the two were wed and headed to Hollywood.

When the couple arrived in the Golden State, Hatton wasted no time contacting his friend Henry King. The director was working on *In Old Chicago* with Tyrone Power, Alice Faye, and Don Ameche. He was pleasantly surprised to hear from his Tampa discovery and gave him a part in the film as a menacing bodyguard. Other roles would follow. He can be seen in *The Hunchback of Notre Dame* (1939), *The Moon and Sixpence* (1942), and *The Oxbow Incident* (1943). He also worked for Henry King in *Alexander's Ragtime Band* (1938), and *Chad Hanna* (1940). Hatton's roles were small and usually uncredited, but his image was unforgettable. His appearance as The Creeper in 1944's *The Pearl of Death,* led to talk of a series of sequels for him and his character beginning with *House of Horrors* in 1946 and *The Brute Man* that same year.

Despite his menacing looks or the way that audiences perceived him, Rondo Hatton had the off-screen reputation of a kind and gentle individual. He understood the plight of wounded veterans and would spend hours visiting the hospitals that cared for them; offering encouragements and humor to those that he felt were giving up emotionally. Harkening back to his days as a student at Tampa's Hillsborough High where he was picked best looking in his class, Hatton would often point to his own distorted features and say;

"Can you believe I once won a beauty contest?"

When he heard that a fifteen-year-old Tampa boy named Bobby Suarez was undergoing surgery in Los Angeles, Hatton spent the day with him at the hospital. It was to be one of his last acts of kindness. Rondo Hatton died on the morning of February 2, 1946, from the pulmonary complications of Acromegaly which caused his heart to enlarge and his blood pressure to reach uncontrollable levels. His body was returned to Tampa and he was given full military honors with members of his unit, the Florida Company H. Rifles serving as pallbearers. He was laid to rest at the American Legion Cemetery.

28

GIBSON GOWLAND
(Henry Morgan)

MR. and Mrs. Gibson Gowland returned to the United States with their son George in 1938; stopping in Tampa to visit Rachelle's family before continuing on to California. The memories of their meeting on the set and their time together under the palm trees must have surely brought about sentimental feelings. Gowland was sixty-one years old and was once again reflecting on his career. The past five years were most trying for him; he had worked in the frigid waters of Greenland to make *S.O.S. Iceberg* and in the steamy jungles of Ceylon to complete *Tea Leaves in the Wind* for the British company Chesterfield Films (*Tea Leaves in the Wind* was renamed *Hate in Paradise* for U.S. distribution). He also appeared in a half dozen movies made at various studios in England.

He gave an interview to the *Tampa Tribune* during his visit and in it, Gowland expounded on his career as a villain and how he played the same character over and over even though, in his opinion, he did not fit the part. He singled out *S.O.S Iceberg* for the harshest comments

"I fought a woman, pushed a guy over an iceberg. I tried to eat a dog, and finally went crazy."

He was looking forward to working in the United States again and even considered obtaining U.S. citizenship. His return to America was a new beginning that ignited within him the possibility of different roles. This time perhaps, with a wife to help raise his son, he could expand as an actor and take on greater parts.

After settling back in Los Angeles, his dreams of a comeback were halted by the cold water splash of reality. He was relegated once again to small, background parts which did not receive an onscreen credit. He plays a villager in *The Wolfman* (1941), a parishioner in *Going My Way* (1944), and a coachman in *The Picture of Dorian Gray* (1945). He worked for Henry King one last time in 1945 playing a senator in *Wilson*. It is disappointing that his appearance in films like *Mrs. Miniver* and *How Green Was My Valley*, where Gowland's British accent might have been a plus, did not call him to larger roles. The actor who was hailed for his performance twenty years earlier as John McTeague in *Greed* and whose riveting portrayal of a character spiraling downward from a successful dentist to a murderous madman was now an unrecognizable bit player lost in the crowd.

By 1948, Gibson Gowland could see that his career was ending, and with his marriage to Rachelle over, he returned to England where he died in 1951.

29

LUPE VELEZ
(Anita)

LUPE Velez returned to Hollywood after *Hell Harbor* and continued working. Her celebrity grew with each film and reported antic. There was, however, a dark and ominous specter that followed Lupe, and it exhibited itself in acts of sometimes senseless and unprovoked violence. In 1931, when her relationship with Gary Cooper ended, she met him at the L.A. train station from where he was departing and fired a shot at him from a small handgun, just missing the actor's head. She married the Olympic swimmer and actor most associated with *Tarzan*, Johnny Weissmuller in 1933. Their six-year marriage ended amid accusations of violence from both parties. While appearing on stage and playing Maria in Cole Porter's musical, *You Never Know,* Lupe blackened the eye of her costar, Libby Holman, bringing an end to the show's troubled 1938 run.

Despite having an almost physically lethal reputation, Lupe was well liked by many in the show business community. She was known to be overly generous to friends and strangers alike. When she was filming *Hell Harbor* in Tampa, she commented on how many calls she accepted from people who needed financial help. On all of her film sets, whenever she completed a scene, the actress preferred to sit with members of the crew, sharing jokes and stories with them. If a new actor or actress was on the set she would read lines and rehearse with them to make them feel welcome.

She was chastised by the Mexican government in 1932 for appearing in *The Broken Wing;* a movie that was deemed so insulting to the people of Mexico that it was banned in that country.

In 1939 she starred in *The Girl From Mexico,* a comedy which featured Lupe as Carmelita Fuentes, a Mexico City singer who falls for an American press agent played by Donald Woods. Lupe's character is assisted in her romantic game of cat and mouse by the uncle of Woods, played by Leon Errol. The movie was so popular that it created a franchise of seven successful films under the *Mexican Spitfire* brand throughout the 1940s.

In the *Mexican Spitfire* series, Carmelita Fuentes becomes Carmelita Lindsey, the wife of Dennis Lindsey. Her vivacious and mischievous personality places her in situations where hilarity ensues; much to the dismay of the staid Lindsey clan and often with the help of Uncle Matt.

1944 brought Lupe Velez back to Mexico for her final film *Nana.* The motion picture was a Mexican production based on the 1880 novel by Emil Zola. As a drama, it was a complete departure for the actress known more for light-hearted, madcap comedies.

Nana tells the story of an actress that earns her money as a prostitute. Nana Coupeau is the "It girl" of Paris, and though she has no discernible talent on the stage, there is an aura of sexual attractiveness around her that is so strong her other shortcomings are overlooked. The person of Nana is hidden by her allure. Men are drawn to her but at the same time, they are blind to her. They cannot see that wrapped in the celestial beauty and charms of a Diana is a simple street-walker whose price is not the wealth they lavish upon her, but their social and financial ruin.

Nana is paid well for her services; she is more of an actress in the life that she lives than she could ever be on the stage. She attains money, but her generosity to those in need keeps her own purse empty. She is incapable of fidelity to any man because her time with men is strictly for commerce. Underneath the calluses that have hardened her heart, there is also love and selflessness that manifests itself at the end.

Shortly after *Nana's* completion, Lupe Velez turned the dark power of violence upon herself. Standing alone after being jilted by her lover, and expecting his child, Lupe adjourned to her bedroom one evening and swallowed seventy-five Seconal tablets with brandy. She was 36.

As she lay in repose, the mourners did not see the Lupe Velez they remembered; a raven-haired beauty full of life and energy. Instead, they saw a young blonde woman who had fought her last fight; her tresses still dyed for her role in *Nana*.

30

PAUL E. BURNS
(Blinky)

PAUL E. Burns passed away at age 86 in Van Nuys, California. His simple sixty-five-word obituary published in the Los Angeles Times on May 19, 1967, listed his profession as a character actor. It failed to mention that he had appeared in over 250 motion pictures and television programs in a film career that started with *Hell Harbor* and ended with a small part in 1967's *Barefoot in the Park*.

He left the fading footlights of Vaudeville behind as a manager, to work for Henry King as a supporting actor. Burns made the character of Blinky all his own and in doing so brought a comic sense of timing to each performance. An example of his talent can be observed in how he saves the poorly written and ill-conceived scene where Blinky is asked to kill Bob Wade. Burns humorously shepherds the situation to a point where the audience becomes so transfixed by the comedy, that the bad joke it is wrapped in, is overlooked. Trying to hide Blinky behind a chair is the gag that steals the scene.

In a long career, Burns played everything from a cowboy in Henry King's 1939 western, *Jesse James* to a Roman in *Spartacus* (1961), usually appearing in roles that were incidental and not given a credit. One of his films, *The Oxbow Incident*, reunited him with his old friend Rondo Hatton, who no doubt chided Burns about his days in Tampa. Hatton had written an article about the actor in Tampa; making good-natured fun of his inability to grow a real beard. Burns also appeared in dozens of television programs during its early years. He never achieved the same level of stardom on film that he experienced in Vaudeville, but he remained a talented, working actor to his last days.

31

GEORGE BOOKASTA
(Spotty)

G EORGE Bookasta never made a movie where he received an onscreen credit after *Hell Harbor*. He did, however, remain in show business, but worked behind the camera. Between 1933 and 1941 he appeared in small mainly walk-on parts, usually as a bellboy or an urchin. In real life, he was a student at Hollywood High School where he was a noted track star.

After high school, he worked in various assistant jobs at Paramount Studios to learn more about the industry, and at night he was a bandleader. As a member of the U.S. Army during World War II, Bookasta was wounded while fighting in France. Upon his return home, he attended Loyola University.

He created and published the magazine *TV Time*, a precursor to *TV Guide*, which gave readers a schedule of television programming for the week. After the sale of his magazine, Bookasta moved to New York and worked as a director for *The Colgate Variety Series*. He went on to direct product commercials throughout the 1960s and 1970s.

George Bookasta retired to Saratoga Springs, New York where he owned and raised horses. He died at age 96 on April 2, 2014

32

JOHN HOLLAND
(Bob Wade)

TWO years after appearing in Hell Harbor, John Holland vanished from Hollywood. The enigmatic actor had appeared in an astonishing sixteen motion pictures in a five year period spanning 1926-1931, and during that time all eyes —particularly those of the fairer sex— were drawn to his on-screen presence where he worked diligently to create characters that were believable and interesting. His greatest challenge came, however, in creating the real-life persona of John Holland.

His given name was James Barham Holland and he was born in Kenosha, Wisconsin. After divorcing, his mother returned to her hometown of Greensboro, North Carolina where she raised her son. Although he was born in Kenosha, Wisconsin, he identified as a country boy from the South. According to his own account, at the age of fifteen he was sent away to boarding school, but in rebelling against the rigidity of the institution, and giving in to his own sense of wanderlust, he ran away to join the Navy. His seaman's career would be cut short, however, after he was discharged for being AWOL.

The Navy had cast Holland adrift at a time when the

world was being engulfed by a geopolitical typhoon. Since 1914, the empires of Europe were falling, borders were changing, and "The War to End All Wars" was decimating a generation of young men. The United States had managed to avoid involvement in the conflict until April of 1917, when Germany's actions forced a breach in America's position of neutrality, thus elevating "The Great War" into World War I.

1918 found James Holland in the Maritime province of New Brunswick, Canada where he volunteered for service in the Canadian Army. Eager to be a part of the fight, he fully expected to sail for Europe, but the tides of war and politics would dictate a different course. His theater of battle would not be in the trenches of Flanders or France, but rather in Russia, and more precisely Siberia, where a new front was opening up and a monumental social upheaval was taking place.

In 1917 Russia was steeped in a civil war between the Communist Bolshevik Red Army and the White Russian Coalition of anti-Communists. Russia had been fighting alongside the Allied Powers against Germany, but after the abdication of Czar Nicholas II, the war-weary nation withdrew from the conflict. In order to make peace with Germany and its allies, Russia's new leader, Vladimir Lenin ceded a large portion of his country's land to its former enemy. This raised fears among the Allies that Russia was tacitly supporting the Kaiser and that supplies previously delivered to Archangelsk for an Eastern Offensive would fall either into enemy hands or into the hands of the equally mistrusted Bolsheviks.

At the behest of Great Britain and the other Allies, The

United States and Canada were asked to provide troops for the Siberian Expedition. The mission of the U.S. would be to guard the port of Archangelsk and its supplies near Norway, while the Canadians would land at Vladivostok in the Far East to provide training and support for the White Russian army.

After four months of military training, James Holland traveled across the vast expanse of Canada by troop train to British Columbia where on December 26; he set sail on the Protesilaus for Siberia. Unlike their American counterparts who saw 500 of their fellow "Polar Bears" fall during firefights with the Red Army; the Canadian contingent's mission was far more peaceful, losing less than twenty men, mostly from influenza. For Holland, it was an unremarkable mission, but he did manage to continue the habit of leaving his post a few times and was reprimanded, although not as severely as his court-martial in the U.S. Navy. He returned to Canada after the Armistice with the rest of his regiment and was discharged on June 10, 1919.

Holland came back to the United States and settled in Norfolk, Virginia to be close to his father who lived in nearby Portsmouth. At some point, the ever-restless young man, who was working as a taxi driver, decided to pursue a theatrical career. He was accepted into Lasky's School for Amateurs, a short-lived training program that scoured the United States for acting talent, and graduated such stars as Charles "Buddy" Rogers and Thelma Todd. The school would ultimately be absorbed into Paramount Studios.

While Holland's good looks did get him an important

audition, his acting ability got him one particularly brutal rejection from the project's casting director; imparting the unvarnished advice that he should never, ever consider acting as a profession. Angry but undeterred, Holland played summer stock and took bit parts where he could find them. He gave himself a timeframe of one year to either learn his craft or heed the casting director's advice.

In 1926, with just a short amount of time left to his deadline, Holland auditioned for the legendary Allen Dwan. Dwan had started as a writer while still attending Notre Dame University and worked at various times as an actor, director, and producer. His storied career spanned five decades and his directorial works include *The Sands of Iwo Jima* (1949) starring John Wayne. Whether it was Holland's improved acting abilities or his stories about Vladivostok, the Canadian- born Dwan hired Holland for the highly visible role of Martin Cole in *Summer Bachelors.*

Holland would follow this film with two more; *Rich but Honest* and *The Secret Studio* where he received top billing as the male lead. His name on the marquee for these films was Clifford Holland. The young actor's career seemed to be on an upward trajectory when suddenly, he was diagnosed with a severe allergic reaction to the make-up used in the movies. At the same time, he also suffered a nervous breakdown and a brain hemorrhage. Holland took a hiatus of two years to recover from his ailments and returned to the screen in 1929 when Henry King cast him as the lead in *She Goes to War.* He had come back into the film industry both physically healthier and mentally reinvigorated. He also returned with a new name: John Holland. His success in *She Goes to War* would lead to another offer by Director Henry King one year later to play the romantic interest of Lupe Velez in *Hell Harbor.*

By 1930, the once would-be actor that was told he would never have a career in motion pictures had returned as a star —and was a prolific one at that, with four movies being released that year including a third collaboration with Henry King, *Eyes of the World.* Five more films would follow in 1931.

To the press, he cultivated his off-screen image as a rootless bachelor that roomed and played at the Hollywood Athletic Club. He was also charmed his interviewers as a Southern gentleman that was always polite, and perhaps even a little naive thus masking the much worldlier man behind the character. On September 13, 1929, *The Tampa Daily Times* reporter Mary Martin interviewed the actor on a number of subjects. When the inevitable question was asked about the handsome leading man's love life, Holland blushingly replied;

"There is a girl in Hollywood who is mighty nice."

The name of the "girl" or what she did in Hollywood was never revealed. Reporter Mary Martin speculated, that given the demeanor of Holland, his lady-friend must have been "A modest girl," who knew "more about home cooking... than home brew." Ten days later, in an article published in the same paper titled *John Holland Approves Looks of Tampa Women* it was reported that Holland was engaged.

A hint to the mystery woman's identity can be found in

the 1930 census that was enumerated on April 7, of that year. In it Holland is listed as married and living on Wonderland Avenue in Hollywood with his wife; the silent film actress Mae Busch. Her father William also lived with the couple. It is understandable why Holland never mentioned his lady friend by name, if it indeed was Busch, because at that time, Busch was still married to her second husband.

Holland also confirmed his bachelor status again in an August 1930 interview granted to Alma Whitaker of the *Los Angeles Times* less than a year after his telling interview in Tampa.

Holland never mentioned having a wife in the 1930 article. Though he did mention that he had recently purchased a new house and that his mother was coming to live with him, there was not, however, one word about a wife. So while he claimed to be married, it appears that the "marriage" was not a legally recognized union, and may have simply been the cohabitation between two people that might or might not have been planning to marry. What is apparent is that their time together was brief, leaving Holland to further cultivate his image of a happy bachelor. Busch went on to play the demanding wife of Oliver Hardy in a number Laurel and Hardy features and remarried in 1936.

Holland began to notice that his name on the movie credits of his films was moving closer to the bottom. While 1931 was a very active year for Holland, his star was beginning to decline. He appeared in five films that year including *Defenders of the Law* which also co-starred Mae Busch, *Ladies Man* with William Powell, Kay Francis, and Carol Lombard, and *Morals for Women.* Watching his name fall on the movie credits list from the main star to a supporting actor made Holland reassess once again his place in the industry.

In the 1930 interview with Alma Whitaker, Holland addressed this change, bemoaning the fact that good parts were not being offered to him. In the article he threatened;

"And let me tell you. If I don't get a good contract by first of the year, I'll spite Hollywood by leaving it cold and going off to see some more of the world."

His last film was the 1932 low budget morality play *The Silver Lining* later renamed, *The Big House for Girls.* In it, John Warburton, a new face on the screen and the same age as Holland, played the romantic lead to Maureen O'Sullivan while Holland, a veteran leading man, was reduced to a bit part.

After this film, the handsome vagabond vanished from the screen, making good on his promise to leave Hollywood flat. He died on September 2, 1971, in Laguna Beach, California; fifty miles and a lifetime away from Hollywood.

31

AL ST. JOHN
(Bunion the Sailor)

WHEN *Hell Harbor's* filming came to an end, Al St. John returned to Hollywood and immediately began working in westerns. The genre would become a specialty for him; so much so that he developed a character named Fuzzy Q. Jones, a grizzled sidekick that appeared in over eighty films between 1937 and 1952.

Fuzzy Q. Jones was more than a role; it was a brand and Fuzzy was everywhere. He was the same sidekick to a number of different White Hat Saturday morning matinee cowboys. Among his costars were Buster Crabbe, Lash LaRue, and George Houston. Because of the low budgets needed to produce these types of movies, the studios could produce more of them and still make a profit. It was, therefore, not unusual to see Fuzzy Q. Jones on a double bill riding with two different heroes. St. John became so quickly associated with the character that he was often billed as "Fuzzy" St John in the credits.

After 1952 when the popularity of the movie serial western declined, Fuzzy hung up his spurs and retired from movies after completing *The Frontier Phantom* with Lash LaRue. He would purchase a ranch in Homosassa Springs,

Florida named the Double F with his fourth wife Flo- Bell
Moore. The homestead was located about 70 miles north of
Tampa.

Though retired from films, St. John began touring with
Ramblin' "Doc" Tommy Scott's Wild West Show. He was in
Leesburg, Florida on January 19, 1963, when he complained
about feeling weak. Always the consummate showman, St.
John went before the audience but performed his entire
act while sitting in a chair. Two days later, he and Flo-Bell
traveled to the South Georgia town of Vidalia, and while
preparing to make a personal appearance, Al St. John suffered
a massive heart attack and died. His remains were delivered
to a mortuary in Macon and cremated. The ashes of the
comedian were given to his wife, who returned to Florida
and deposited them in the tranquil ground of the Double F
Ranch.

32

ROBERT HAAS
(Art Director)

ROBERT Haas continued to excel as an Art Director. His work defined the look of some of Hollywood's most important movies of the 1930s and 1940s which have, in turn, inspired countless generations of art directors. In *Angels with Dirty Faces* (1938), he contrasted the teeming slums of New York with the stark prison cells of Death Row; making James Cagney's cowardly cry for mercy even more powerful. He was called upon twice to design sets for The Maltese Falcon: Once for the original 1931 version and again, ten years later, for its better-known remake.

His work served as a backdrop for Bette Davis in five of her finest performances: *Jezebel* (1938), *The Old Maid* (1939), *Dark Victory* (1939), *Now Voyager* (1942) and *Mr. Skeffington* (1944). Whether Haas was assigned to a motion picture about the 1890s or the 1950s his exacting attention to the slightest details regarding the architecture and interiors of the period transformed the soundstages of Hollywood into exceedingly accurate depictions of their stories time and place.

Haas would be nominated for two Academy Awards; *Life with Father* (1948) in color and Johnny Belinda (1950) in black and white. His last film was *The Glass Menagerie* in 1950 starring Kirk Douglas and Jane Wyman. Haas died in 1962.

33

ERNEST ROVERE
(Sound)

AFTER *Hell Harbor,* Ernest Rovere immediately went to work on Henry King's next picture, *The Eyes of the World.* The movie reunited him with cameraman John P. Fulton and Editor, Lloyd Nosler. N. Brewster Morse wrote the screenplay which was adapted by Clarke Silvernail from a novel the same name.

Rovere did the sound work for a short feature titled *High Hats and Low Brows* in 1932. It was to be his last film before he embarked on an entirely new career as a professional Contract Bridge player. His enthusiasm for the card game was unmatched and he encouraged its play at every opportunity. The ex-sound engineer brought a current of electricity to the game that had been mainly confined to senior citizen parlors and widened its appeal.

Ernest Rovere published a daily syndicated newspaper column on the subject for many years and served as the Bridge Editor of the San Francisco Chronicle. The Public Broadcasting System carried his instructional television program and radio stations broadcast his discussions on strategy. He also was the author of a number of definitive books on the subject. When he was not playing in tournaments throughout the United States, he was teaching seminars and organizing ocean cruises with the game as its focus. In 1948 he was named the 100th person with the title of Life Master.

He died in 2000 at the age of 95.

34

EUGENE BERTON
(Composer)

EUGENE Berton died in 1969 and at the time, the classically trained baritone was working as a voice teacher for aspiring singers. In his youth, he had been educated by some of Europe's most notable talents in the art of piano and voice. He had been brought to them because of his natural abilities to play piano by ear and the projection of his vocal intonations. Prior to such lofty educational opportunities, he had been a Vaudeville star starting at age six. As he grew older he became interested in classical piano and proved to be somewhat of a prodigy.

The Berton brothers were all musically inclined. The oldest brother Vic had made his mark on the Jazz circuit playing with such luminaries as Roger Wolfe Kahn and Bix Beiderbecke. He was eventually hired by Paramount Studios and served as its musical director for a brief time.

Eugene joined his brother in California after a successful career as a classical singer. Shortly after his arrival in Hollywood, he was offered the opportunity to write the music for *Hell Harbor,* the only film for which he would receive an onscreen credit. Sadly, his name —like that of Lecuona's would also be misspelled on the opening titles; appearing as Eugene Berten.

Disillusioned by the movie industry, Eugene returned to Pennsylvania where he became interested in the music of the stage and show tunes. In the 1950's he collaborated with his younger brother Ralph to create a modern version of Puccini's *La Boheme* set among the beatniks. It played briefly off-Broadway and was never to be seen again. A later foray into musical theatre also proved to be disastrous for him.

Eugene Berton never achieved the stature that his potential had expected of him. As a child, he had a successful career in Vaudeville. As a young man, he gained a reputation as a classical singer that performed with some of the most respected symphonies in the United States. His star though began to fade upon his arrival in Hollywood. Berton's work providing the music for *Hell Harbor* is his greatest and only cinematic achievement of note during this time. *Caribbean Love Song* became his musical legacy, his opus, and his swan song.

35

MACK STENGLER AND
JOHN P. FULTON
(Cameramen)

THE photography that made *Hell Harbor* visually astounding in both its clarity and beauty is attributed to the camera work of Stengler and Fulton.

Mack Stengler and Henry King never worked together again after *Hell Harbor*, but Stengler went on to have a long career behind the camera. While some of the stories that he captured on film were less than stellar, like *The Terror of Tiny Town* (1938) and *Freckles Comes Home* (1942), they were photographed with professionalism. In 1949 he turned his attention to the new medium of television; bringing many classic programs to viewers for the first time in the early days of the technology.

Stengler photographed nearly every episode of *The Lone Ranger*. He also worked on various installments of *Hopalong Cassidy*, *Gunsmoke*, *The Millionaire*, *The Jack Benny Program*, *The Liberace Show*, and *Leave it to Beaver*. The very first airing of *The Lawrence Welk Show* was shot by Stengler in 1955. Unlike his time in the movies, where he never received an industry accolade, his work on television earned a Primetime

Emmy Award for Best Cinematography for *Day of Glory;* an
episode that aired on *Jane Wyman Presents the Fireside Theater*
in 1958.

Mack Stengler died in 1962 and was buried at the San
Gabriel Mission Cemetery in Los Angeles, California.

****

Upon the completion of *Hell Harbor,* John P. Fulton
was hired to film *The Eyes of the World* for Henry King in
California. Fulton saw cinematography as an art. His father
was Fitch Fulton, a gifted Nebraska born artist known for oil
paintings and colorful landscapes. The elder Fulton had also
worked as a matte painter on *Gone with the Wind* and *Citizen
Kane.* His design of landscapes and interiors on canvas helped
create the illusion of an actual location. His son, John saw
celluloid as his canvas and used it to exaggerate live action
through the power of special effects.

His camera work continues to impress generations
of moviegoers. No one can be so jaded by modern special
effects as to not be amazed when Claude Rains removes his
bandages in *The Invisible Man* made in 1932. There is still
a sense of awe when Moses parts the Red Sea in Cecil B.
DeMille's 1956 version of *The Ten Commandments,* or when
viewing James Stewart's fist clenching scenes of psychological
terror in *Vertigo.*

John Fulton's use of photography did not just enhance a
movie; it defined it. He created scenes so memorable that they
are often the first recollection of the film whenever the title is

simply mentioned. His work impressed some of Hollywood's most unflappable directors and names like Alfred Hitchcock and William Wyler, clamored to make films with him.

In a career that spanned forty years, Fulton produced effects for over 250 movies, many of which were made while he was head of the Special Effects Department at Paramount for nearly a decade starting in 1953. Over the years his work was nominated for eight Academy Awards and he won three of them for; *Wonder Man* (1945), *The Bridges at Toko-Ri* (1955), and *The Ten Commandments* (1956).

He died of a blood infection while working on *The Battle of Britain* in 1967.

36

N. BREWSTER MORSE
(Scenario Writer)

ON March 2, 1930, Myra Nye's column, *Society of Cinemaland* reported in the *Los Angeles Times* that N. Brewster Morse had hosted a luncheon for Jerome Adler and his wife at the Roosevelt Hotel. Adler was the largest pearl importer in the United States and a dear friend of Morse's father who was Vice President of Tiffany & Company. The conversation over lunch most assuredly included *Hell Harbor*, and how it begins with the sale of pearls. The movie had not yet premiered in New York so after lunch, Morse brought everyone over to Tec-Art Studios for a tour.

At twenty-seven, the young writer was plying his trade in Hollywood but sales were difficult. His script for *Eyes of the World* was in production with Henry King directing, but he did not have any other script in the pipeline and was continuing to write. *The Savage Girl,* a low budget movie with a screenplay by Morse was released in 1932. In 1938 he co-wrote *The Perfect Specimen* starring Errol Flynn. Although he was finding it difficult to sell his screenplays, his short stories were still in demand for adaptation. In 1938 *Breaking the Ice* was purchased as a vehicle to showcase the talents of the young Canadian born singer Bobby Breen and his even younger co-star; the ice skater Irene Dare. The last Morse story purchased for a film was *The Lady with Red Hair*, starring Miriam Hopkins as the turn of the century actress, Mrs. Leslie Carter in 1940.

Finding work in films difficult to obtain, Morse returned to the theater. His comedy *Brass Wings*, about a college student, and a showgirl was performed at the Hollytown Theater in April of 1942. The little community theater located in the heart of the movie industry was a proving ground for new actors and playwrights. The leading man in *Brass Wings* was personally selected by Morse and the play met an enthusiastic reception from its audiences.

Six months later, on October 20, 1942, Morse joined the United States Army and married his second wife ten days later. When he returned to civilian life, he attempted to return to show business as a producer. N. Brewster Morse Productions, Inc., announced in 1946, that it was planning a biographical motion picture on the life of singer Russ Columbo with Beatrice Kay named as the leading lady. The film, however, was never made.

By the end of the 1950s, the once-talented poet, playwright, and scion of wealth and privilege was living in the economically declining Pico-Union District of Los Angeles while amassing a growing collection of rejection letters. He suffered a stroke on February 10, 1958, and was admitted into the Los Angeles County Hospital where he would die eleven days later at the age of 64.

37

FREDERIQUE DE GRESAC
(Screenwriter)

FREDERIQUE de Gresac died on Friday, February 19, 1943, and with her ended an epoch that joined film and theater together. At the time of her death, much of the talent that was arriving in Hollywood came without the experience of working on or writing for the stage. Their points of reference were now moviemakers and not stage directors. The acting was less physically dramatic because of sound, and the emotional portrayals became more subtle. Movies were creating their own art form, which was distinctly separate from stagecraft.

The last film she adapted was *Hell Harbor* and while she continued to write, her screen presence was fading. In 1938 MGM brought *Sweethearts* to the screen with Nelson Eddy and Jeanette McDonald in the title roles. Writers Dorothy Parker and Allen Campbell drastically changed the play's storyline from that of the original Broadway play. Frederique de Gresac's story about a child princess hiding and working in a laundry while her nation is in turmoil becomes the story of Broadway stars falling in and out of love. The only recognizable parts of the play were the lyrics she wrote to Victor Herbert's music.

The Parisian writer that was unsung because of her sex put a song on the lips of America. Her talent made her a commanding presence on the stages of Broadway and the soundstages of Hollywood.

38

CLARKE SILVERNAIL
(Dialogue Screenwriter)

CLARKE Silvernail's determination to succeed as a writer in Hollywood is exemplified in his cross country trip to Tampa while confined to a bed. He viewed writing the dialogue for *Hell Harbor* as an important task and he went to the set every day even though he was often forced to rest after short periods of exertion in the hot sun. The public was told that he had malaria, but the physical weakness he experienced was a symptom of the cancer that would take his life one year later.

Silvernail had one more screenplay produced after *Hell Harbor*. It was a Western titled *Shadow Ranch,* starring Buck Jones and directed by Louis King, Henry's brother. The movie was released on September 28, 1930, but the young writer would not live to see its distribution; he would die six days earlier at his home in Los Angeles.

As an impassioned member of Actor's Equity in New York, he worked unsuccessfully to organize the stars of the film industry in California. When he was not espousing the virtues of unionization to those that would listen, he was writing. Along with the two films he wrote for Henry King:

Hell Harbor and the now lost *Eyes of the World,* his work also includes the 1929 murder mystery *Behind That Curtain* which introduced Detective Charlie Chan to audiences.

The tragedy of his short life in Hollywood, aside from leaving a young son, was that he never had the chance to achieve the same level of success as a writer that he had on Broadway, working as an actor and director. His contributions to *Hell Harbor* are often judged more harshly than they should be yet, reflecting on the three existing films that bear his name, Clarke Silvernail proves that he was able to master any assignment given to him.

39

H ELL Harbor, the movie and Rida Johnson-Young, the writer whose novel inspired it, have suffered the same fate: A lack of recognition.

Just as Johnson-Young wrote songs and lyrics so popular they are recognized as standards over a century later; few associate her name with them. The same lack of recognition also befalls the technical feats of *Hell Harbor*. Modern movie audiences have become accustomed to exotic locations, clear and understandable dialogue, and flawless sound mixing that includes or discards background noises that affect the scene. Very few, however, can trace those obvious elements to the film that first used them. While commonplace and expected today; in 1929 these were groundbreaking innovations.

The movie is a record of the early technical achievements in sound and camera work, but it is also a time capsule; forever storing within it a moment in time. *Hell Harbor* retains the youthful pulchritude of a twenty-two-year-old Lupe Velez; the tough Northumberland accent of a rarely heard Gibson Gowland and the Vaudeville-like antics of Paul Burns and Al St. John. The film gives witness to a moment in the short career of John Holland, and a new beginning in the long career of Jean Hersholt. The local extras: long gone by the morbid call of destiny, remain forever young, alive and beaming with excitement on the celluloid frames of the film.

Hell Harbor today may look and feel old. The sound,

when compared to modern techniques of recording, appears adequate but dated. The dialogue is at times corny and some of the short moments of slapstick seem out of place. Yet, its importance as a mark in cinematic history cannot be understated.

One aspect of *Hell Harbor* that does stand the test of time is its photography. Mack Stengler and John P. Fulton present Rocky Point as it will never be again; their shots of Tampa Bay's shimmering waters depict the never changing beauty of the open sea and sky. Yet, within the 35mm time capsule, there is —unseen— the nuanced eternity of Tampa, found in the flickering frames of *Hell Harbor*.

ACKNOWLEDGEMENTS

THIS book could not come to a conclusion without recognizing the invaluable assistance of Dr. Matthew Knight, Director of Special Collections at the University of South Florida Library. His help and support provided access to research materials that gave greater depth and understanding to the story, which ultimately allowed me to write a better book.

The staff of the John F. Germany Library of the Tampa-Hillsborough County Public Library System deserves praise because of their everyday work as a repository of words and artifacts that assures an understanding of the city's past.

An equal level of gratitude goes out to the reporters of the St. Petersburg Times, The Tampa Daily Times, and the Tampa Tribune who between June 1929 and January 1930 diligently chronicled the events of Hell Harbor's production. Some worked with a byline; some with a nom de plume; and some even worked anonymously, but all —though they may not have recognized it at the time— contributed indelibly to the history of their area.

Archival copies of The Milford Dispatch and Pike County Press, The Brooklyn Daily Eagle, The New York Times, The Los Angeles Times, The Des Moines Register, The New York Herald, and The New York American were instrumental in giving a wider view of *Hell Harbor's* reach and texture as a motion picture.

Much thanks to The Internet Movie Database and the Internet Broadway Database for their unmatched compilation of facts, dates, and information about their subjects.

Finally, I must thank the many friends and family that patiently listened as I spoke enthusiastically of a film they never saw, actors of which they never heard, and a time that they never lived in. I hope this book clears it all up.

ABOUT THE AUTHOR

KEVIN J. Martinez graduated from the University of South Florida with a B.A.in Political Science, and would go on to build a career as a financial advisor specializing in the options market. In 2011 he authored *The Book on Put Option Writing*, which detailed the mechanizations and strategies involved in selling equity contracts.

Kevin is a Life Member of the University of South Florida Alumni Association and has served as president to a number of civic organizations. A voracious reader and movie enthusiast, he is currently working on his next writing project.